CREATIVITY , INNOVATION & BUSINESS DEVELOPMENT

A GUIDE BASED ON CALICUT UNIVERSITY BBA - MDC FIRST SEMESTER FYUGP CURRICULAM

AF582378

PRASY PADMANABHAN

Copyright © PRASY PADMANABHAN
All Rights Reserved.

This book has been self-published with all reasonable efforts taken to make the material error-free by the author. No part of this book shall be used, reproduced in any manner whatsoever without written permission from the author, except in the case of brief quotations embodied in critical articles and reviews.

The Author of this book is solely responsible and liable for its content including but not limited to the views, representations, descriptions, statements, information, opinions and references ["Content"]. The Content of this book shall not constitute or be construed or deemed to reflect the opinion or expression of the Publisher or Editor. Neither the Publisher nor Editor endorse or approve the Content of this book or guarantee the reliability, accuracy or completeness of the Content published herein and do not make any representations or warranties of any kind, express or implied, including but not limited to the implied warranties of merchantability, fitness for a particular purpose. The Publisher and Editor shall not be liable whatsoever for any errors, omissions, whether such errors or omissions result from negligence, accident, or any other cause or claims for loss or damages of any kind, including without limitation, indirect or consequential loss or damage arising out of use, inability to use, or about the reliability, accuracy or sufficiency of the information contained in this book.

Made with ♥ on the Notion Press Platform
www.notionpress.com

Contents

Course Summary & Course Outcomes

Course Summary

This course explores the intersections of creativity, innovation, and business development, focusing on how these elements combine to spark new ideas, drive technological advancements, and create sustainable business models in a competitive global marketplace. Students will engage with concepts from design thinking, lean startup methodologies, and disruptive innovation theories to understand how businesses can innovate products, services, and processes. Through a blend of lectures, case studies, hands-on projects, and guest speakers, participants will learn to harness their creative potential, apply innovative thinking, and develop practical strategies for business growth and development.

Course Outcomes

CO1:Enable the learner to understand the concept and meaning of creativity, and its importance in various domains, including business

CO2:Enable the learner to identify and develop creativity skills and personal qualities necessary for fostering innovation

CO3:Enable the learner to use creativity tools and techniques

CO4:Enable the learner to understand the concept and types of innovation, the relationship between creativity and innovation, and the role of innovation in business development.

CO5:Enable the learner to analyse the characteristics of successful entrepreneurs and understand the entrepreneurship process and the concept of a business model.

CO6:Enable the learner to explore and evaluate the role of agencies for innovation in Kerala and their contributions to promoting entrepreneurship and innovation.

Syllabus

MODULE 1:

Understanding Creativity Creativity – Nature, Concepts and Meaning.Creativity skills & personal qualities. Role of creativity in business. Techniques to foster creativity: Brainstorming Role Playing,Incubation ,Creativity tools and techniques: SCAMPER , Mind Mapping

MODULE 2

Innovation and its Role in Business- Meaning, Nature, Types of innovation, Relationship between creativity and innovation – Differences Relationship between creativity and innovation – Similarities, Role of innovation in business development. Barriers to innovation, Ways to overcome the barriers.

MODULE 3

Introduction to Entrepreneurship-Meaning Nature and concepts of entrepreneurship, Meaning Nature and concepts of intrapreneurship, Characteristics of successful entrepreneurs, Entrepreneurship Process, Concept of Business Model, Importance of Entrepreneurship Ecosystem, Importance of Entrepreneurship for Economic Development

MODULE 4

Business Development through Entrepreneurship- Steps in starting a new venture and entrepreneurship challenges, Idea generation, Evaluation, and Opportunity Assessment, Business Plan – Concepts, Business Plan – Components, Business Plan – Importance Entrepreneurial Marketing and Financing a New Venture

MODULE 5:Open Ended Module

K-DISC, KIED, Kerala Startup Mission, National Innovation Foundation, Innovation and Entrepreneurship Development Centres, etc.

CHAPTER ONE

UNDERSTANDING CREATIVITY

Meaning and Definition of creativity

Creativity is a process by which a symbolic domain in the culture is changed. Creativity is often celebrated as one of the most profound and transformative human capabilities. At its core, creativity is the process of generating novel and valuable ideas, perspectives, or solutions. It is the spark that drives innovation, artistry, and problem-solving across various domains, from technological advancements to literary masterpieces. Creativity thrives on the ability to see the world through a unique lens, connecting disparate elements in unexpected ways. Whether it manifests in a ground breaking scientific discovery, an evocative piece of art or a clever solution to a complex problem, creativity is fundamental to human progress and expression. As we delve into the essence of creativity, we uncover not just a skill or talent, but a dynamic interplay of imagination, inspiration, and exploration that fuels our collective advancement and personal fulfilment. Creativity is the ability to make or otherwise bring into existences something new, whether a new solution to a problem, a new method or device, or a new artistic object or form. Wyckoff (1991) defines creativity as new and useful. Creativity is the act of seeing things that everyone around us sees while making connections that no one else has made. Creativity is moving from the known to the unknown.

Creativity is the ability to generate new and original ideas, solutions, or approaches. It involves thinking outside the box, making connections between seemingly unrelated concepts, and expressing oneself in unique ways. Creativity can manifest in various forms, including art, science, problem-solving, and everyday activities. It's often driven by curiosity, imagination, and a willingness to take risks or challenge conventional thinking. While it can be an inherent trait for some, creativity can also be nurtured and developed through practice and exploration.

The meaning of creativity extends beyond just artistic or intellectual endeavors; it touches various facets of life:

- **Self-Expression**: Creativity provides a medium for individuals to express their unique perspectives, emotions, and ideas. Whether through art, writing, or personal projects, creativity allows for personal expression and identity formation.
- **Problem-Solving**: Creativity plays a crucial role in addressing complex problems. It involves thinking innovatively to find effective solutions and overcome challenges, whether in scientific research, business strategies, or everyday life.
- **Cultural Advancement**: Throughout history, creativity has driven cultural and societal progress. Artistic, scientific, and technological innovations have shaped civilizations, reflecting the evolving values and aspirations of societies.
- **Personal Fulfillment**: Engaging in creative activities can lead to a sense of satisfaction and accomplishment. It can enhance personal well-being and contribute to a fulfilling life by providing opportunities for growth, learning, and exploration.

Nature of Creativity

Creativity is an intricate and dynamic process that manifests as the ability to generate new and valuable ideas or solutions. It is both a cognitive and emotional phenomenon, deeply embedded in our thinking patterns and influenced by our experiences and environment. Here are some key aspects of the nature of creativity:

Originality: Creativity is marked by the novelty of ideas. Originality involves producing something that is new and distinct from existing concepts. This can apply to artistic works, scientific theories, or everyday problem-solving.

Value: For something to be deemed creative, it must also hold value. This value can be practical, aesthetic, or intellectual. An idea that is original but lacks relevance or utility may not be considered truly creative.

Process-Oriented: Creativity is not just about the final product but also about the process. It involves stages like preparation, incubation, illumination, and verification. This process-oriented view highlights that creativity is as much about the journey of idea development as it is about the outcome.

Contextual Dependence: Creativity often depends on the context in which it occurs. Cultural, social, and environmental factors play a significant role in shaping and influencing creative expressions.

Fluidity and Flexibility: Creativity is characterized by the ability to adapt and shift thinking fluidly. Creative individuals can navigate between different modes of thought and are adept at modifying their approaches as new information or challenges arise. This flexibility allows them to explore diverse avenues and adjust strategies in dynamic contexts.

Complex Interplay of Factors: Creativity arises from the interaction of various factors, including cognitive processes, emotional states, and environmental conditions. It's not just about individual talent but also about how these factors converge to produce innovative outcomes. For instance, a supportive environment can significantly enhance creative potential by providing resources and encouragement.

Role of Intuition: Intuition plays a significant role in the creative process. Often, creative insights emerge spontaneously, without a conscious awareness of the underlying reasoning. This intuitive aspect allows for sudden breakthroughs and novel connections that may not be easily explained through logical reasoning alone.

Incremental vs. Radical Innovation: Creativity can manifest as incremental improvements or radical innovations. Incremental creativity involves gradual enhancements and refinements to existing ideas or products, while radical creativity leads to ground breaking changes that disrupt established paradigms. Both types of creativity are valuable and contribute differently to progress and development.

Theories of Creativity

Several theories provide insights into how creativity functions:

Psychodynamic Theory: Suggests that creativity emerges from the unconscious mind and is influenced by internal conflicts and desires. This theory emphasizes the role of intuition and subconscious processes in creative thought.

Cognitive Theory: Focuses on the mental processes involved in creativity, such as problem-solving strategies and cognitive flexibility. It explores how creative thinking involves both convergent and divergent cognitive processes.

Humanistic Theory: Emphasizes the role of personal growth and self-actualization in creativity. According to this perspective, creativity is a manifestation of an individual's quest for personal fulfilment and self-expression.

Social-Cultural Theory: Highlights the impact of social and cultural factors on creativity. This theory examines how cultural norms, social interactions, and collaborative environments influence creative outcomes.

Creativity Skills & Personal Qualities

1. Divergent Thinking

Divergent thinking is the ability to generate a wide array of possible solutions or ideas for a given problem. It involves brainstorming and free association. It requires breaking away from traditional thinking patterns to explore multiple possibilities. This skill helps in overcoming cognitive biases and fosters an open-ended exploration of ideas. Used in the initial stages of problem-solving or ideation processes, such as brainstorming sessions or creative writing exercises. It's crucial for discovering new opportunities and developing innovative solutions.

2. Convergent Thinking

The ability to narrow down multiple ideas to find the most effective solution is known as convergent thinking, which involves evaluating and synthesizing information to select the best possible outcome. It includes assessing feasibility, practicality, and alignment with objectives.Essential in decision-making processes where numerous options are considered, such as during the refinement phase of a project or when choosing among various creative concepts.

3. Problem-Solving Skills

The capability to identify, analyze, and address complex issues using creative approaches.This skill involves breaking down a problem into manageable parts, identifying potential solutions, and implementing strategies effectively. It requires both analytical and creative thinking to develop innovative solutions. Important in any scenario that involves overcoming obstacles or finding new ways to achieve goals, such as in business strategy, product development, or personal challenges.

4. Analytical Thinking

The ability to systematically evaluate information and identify patterns or connections.Analytical thinking involves critical evaluation of data, logical reasoning, and the ability to deconstruct complex problems. It supports creativity by providing a structured approach to understanding and developing ideas.Useful in analyzing creative projects, evaluating the feasibility of ideas, and ensuring that solutions are grounded in reality. This skill is vital for refining and validating creative concepts.

5. Imaginative Visualization

The ability to mentally create and manipulate images or scenarios. Imaginative visualization helps in conceptualizing abstract ideas and envisioning potential outcomes. It enhances creativity by allowing individuals to explore how ideas might look or function in real-world scenarios. Employed in design and planning processes, such as visualizing a new product, crafting a story, or planning a marketing campaign. It aids in communicating ideas and foreseeing practical applications.

6. Adaptability

The ability to adjust thinking and strategies in response to new information or changing conditions. Adaptability involves being flexible and open to change, which is crucial for navigating dynamic environments and overcoming unexpected challenges. It supports creative thinking by allowing individuals to pivot and explore new directions. Essential in environments where rapid changes occur, such as in startups or creative industries. It helps in adjusting strategies, experimenting with new approaches, and embracing innovation.

7. Technical Skills

Proficiency in specific tools, techniques, or knowledge areas relevant to a field or project.Technical skills enhance the execution of creative ideas by providing the necessary expertise and capabilities. They include skills related to software, artistic techniques, or specialized knowledge. Critical in fields that require specific expertise, such as graphic design, software development, or scientific research. Technical skills ensure that creative ideas can be effectively implemented and refined.

Personal Qualities of creativity

1. Curiosity

An innate desire to explore, learn, and understand new things.Curiosity drives individuals to seek out new experiences, ask questions, and engage with a wide range of topics. It fuels the quest for knowledge and encourages the exploration of novel ideas.Enhances the breadth and depth of creative thinking by fostering a mindset that values exploration and discovery. It leads to a richer understanding of various domains and inspires innovative thinking.

2. Open-Mindedness

The willingness to consider and embrace diverse perspectives and ideas is Open-mindedness ,involves being receptive to new and unconventional ideas, even if they challenge existing beliefs or norms. It promotes a culture of inclusivity and encourages the exploration of different viewpoints. Supports creative problem-solving by allowing for a broader range of ideas and approaches. It helps in overcoming cognitive biases and fosters collaboration and innovation.

3. Risk-Taking

It is the readiness to take chances and venture into uncertain or unfamiliar territory. Risk-taking involves stepping out of one's comfort zone and embracing the possibility of failure as a learning opportunity. It encourages experimentation and the pursuit of bold ideas. Drives innovation by pushing boundaries and exploring uncharted territories. It enables individuals to take on challenges that can lead to significant breakthroughs and advancements.

4. Resilience

The ability to recover from setbacks and persist in the face of challenges is resilience and involves maintaining motivation and determination despite difficulties or failures. It requires emotional strength and a positive attitude towards overcoming obstacles Resilience helps individuals to keep refining their ideas and pursuing their goals with persistence.

5. Self-Confidence

Belief in one's own abilities and judgment.Self-confidence enables individuals to trust their creative instincts and take ownership of their ideas. It fosters a proactive attitude and the courage to share and defend one's work. It Supports the development and communication of creative ideas. Self-confidence empowers individuals to seek feedback, make decisions, and lead creative projects.

6. Passion and Enthusiasm

A strong emotional drive and commitment to creative pursuits. Passion involves a deep interest and dedication to a creative endeavor. Enthusiasm fuels sustained effort and engagement, making the creative process more enjoyable and productive. Motivates individuals to invest time and energy into their creative projects. Passion and enthusiasm contribute to a positive mindset and drive the pursuit of excellence.

7. Empathy

The ability to understand and relate to the emotions and perspectives of others. Empathy helps in designing solutions that address the needs and preferences of others. It involves putting oneself in another's shoes and considering their experiences and challenges.it enhances creativity by ensuring that solutions are relevant and user-centered. Empathy leads to more meaningful and impactful creative outcomes that resonate with diverse audiences.

8. *Playfulness*

An inclination to approach tasks with a sense of fun, exploration, and experimentation. Playfulness encourages a relaxed and open-minded approach to problem-solving. It involves experimenting with new ideas and techniques without fear of failure. Facilitates creativity by creating an environment where unconventional ideas can be explored and enjoyed. Playfulness fosters innovation and can lead to unexpected and exciting discoveries.

9. *Attention to Detail*

The ability to notice and address the finer aspects of a project or idea.Attention to detail involves careful observation and meticulousness in execution. It ensures that all aspects of a creative project are considered and refined. It leads to higher-quality outcomes by ensuring that ideas are well-developed and thoroughly vetted. Attention to detail contributes to the professionalism and effectiveness of creative work.

10. *Patience*

The capacity to take time and maintain focus on long-term creative processes. Patience involves understanding that creative processes often require time and perseverance. It supports sustained effort and careful development of ideas.Allows individuals to work through iterative processes and refine their ideas over time. Patience is essential for achieving depth and quality in creative projects.

Understanding and developing these creativity skills and personal qualities can significantly enhance one's ability to generate innovative ideas and effectively bring them to fruition. Each element contributes to different aspects of the creative process, from ideation and problem-solving to execution and refinement.

The principles of creativity

People become more creative when they feel motivated primarily by the interest, satisfaction, and challenge of the situation and not by external pressures; the passion and interest – a person's internal desire to do something unique to show-case himself or herself; the person's sense of challenge, or a drive to crack a problem that no one else has been able to solve. Within every individual, creativity is a function of three components:

1. Expertise
2. Creative thinking skills
3. Motivation.

Expertise encompasses everything that a person knows and can do in the broad domain of his or her work- knowledge and technical ability. Creative thinking refers to how you approach problems and solutions- the capacity to put existing ideas together in new combinations. The skill itself depends quite a bit on personality as well as on how a person thinks and works. Expertise and creative thinking are the entrepreneur's raw materials or natural resources. Motivation is the drive and desire to do something, an inner passion and interest. When people are intrinsically motivated, they engage in their work for the challenge and enjoyment of it. The work itself is motivating. People will be most creative when they feel motivated primarily by the interest, satisfaction and the challenge of the work itself-"the labour of love", love of the work- "the enjoyment of seeing and searching for an outstanding solution – a break through. Creativity, according to Robert Gahim, consists of anticipation and commitment. Anticipation involves having a vision of something that will become important in the future before anybody else has it. Commitment is the belief that keeps one working to realize the vision despite doubt and discouragement.

Role of Creativity in Business

1. Innovation and Product Development

- **New Products and Services**: Creativity is essential for designing and developing new products and services that meet emerging needs or create new market opportunities. Innovative products often stem from creative thinking, which identifies gaps in the market and conceptualizes solutions that stand out from the competition.
- **Product Differentiation**: In saturated markets, creativity helps businesses differentiate their products from competitors. Creative approaches to product features, design, and packaging can make a product more appealing and unique, enhancing its marketability.
- **Enhancing Existing Offerings**: Creativity isn't limited to new products; it also involves improving existing ones. Creative modifications can lead to better functionality, user experience, or aesthetic appeal, keeping products relevant and competitive.

2. *Marketing and Branding*

- **Innovative Campaigns**: Creativity drives the development of impactful marketing campaigns that capture attention and engage audiences. Creative marketing strategies, such as unique advertising concepts or viral content, can significantly boost brand visibility and customer interest.
- **Brand Identity**: Establishing a strong and memorable brand identity requires creativity. This includes designing logos, developing brand messaging, and creating visual elements that resonate with the target audience and convey the brand's values and personality.
- **Customer Engagement**: Creative approaches to customer engagement, such as interactive content, gamification, or personalized experiences, can foster stronger connections with customers and enhance brand loyalty.

3. *Problem-Solving and Strategy*

- **Creative Problem-Solving**: Businesses often face complex challenges that require innovative solutions. Creativity enables teams to think outside conventional frameworks, explore alternative approaches, and develop effective strategies to address issues.

- **Strategic Planning**: Developing a successful business strategy involves anticipating future trends and adapting to changing conditions. Creative thinking helps in envisioning new business models, exploring market opportunities, and crafting strategies that differentiate the company from its competitors.

4. *Organizational Culture and Leadership*

- **Fostering a Creative Culture**: Encouraging creativity within an organization creates an environment where employees feel empowered to share ideas and experiment. A culture that values creativity promotes collaboration, open communication, and a willingness to take risks.
- **Leadership and Vision**: Creative leadership involves inspiring and guiding teams towards innovative goals. Leaders who embrace and promote creativity can drive organizational change, motivate employees, and lead their businesses to new heights.

5. *Customer Experience and Service*

- **Enhanced Customer Experience**: Creativity in designing customer interactions and service processes can significantly improve the overall customer experience. This includes developing unique service offerings, creating memorable touchpoints, and personalizing customer interactions.
- **Service Innovation**: Creative approaches to service delivery can lead to more efficient and effective ways of meeting customer needs. For example, innovative customer service platforms or processes can streamline interactions and enhance satisfaction.

6. *Competitive Advantage*

- **Market Differentiation**: Creativity helps businesses stand out in a crowded marketplace. Unique and innovative products, services, or marketing strategies can create a distinct competitive edge and attract customers who are looking for something different.
- **Adaptability and Agility**: Creative thinking supports businesses in adapting to market changes and emerging trends. By being open to new ideas and flexible in their approach, companies can quickly respond to shifts in consumer preferences or industry developments.

7. Operational Efficiency

- **Process Improvement**: Creativity can lead to innovative ways of streamlining business operations and improving efficiency. This includes developing new workflows, automating repetitive tasks, and finding cost-effective solutions to operational challenges.
- **Resource Optimization**: Creative approaches to resource management can optimize the use of time, money, and personnel. By rethinking how resources are allocated and utilized, businesses can enhance productivity and reduce waste.

8. Employee Motivation and Retention

- **Engaging Work Environment**: A creative work environment fosters employee engagement and satisfaction. Opportunities for creative expression, involvement in innovative projects, and recognition for creative contributions can boost morale and motivation.
- **Talent Attraction**: Companies known for their creativity and innovation are often more attractive to top talent. Prospective employees are drawn to workplaces that offer opportunities for growth, challenge, and creative expression.

9. Strategic Partnerships and Collaboration

- **Collaborative Innovation**: Creativity enhances the potential for successful partnerships and collaborations. By bringing together diverse perspectives and ideas, businesses can co-create solutions that leverage the strengths of each partner.
- **Network Expansion**: Creative approaches to networking and building relationships can open doors to new opportunities, markets, and resources. Innovative strategies for collaboration can lead to mutually beneficial outcomes and business growth.

10. Long-Term Sustainability

- **Future-Proofing**: Creative thinking helps businesses anticipate and prepare for future challenges. By innovating and exploring new possibilities, companies can stay ahead of industry trends and ensure long-term sustainability.
- **Sustainable Practices**: Creativity can drive the development of environmentally friendly and socially responsible practices. Innovative solutions for sustainability can enhance a company's reputation and appeal to increasingly conscientious consumers.

creativity plays a pivotal role in driving innovation, improving processes, enhancing customer experiences, and building a strong organizational culture. By integrating creativity into various aspects of business, companies can achieve greater success, maintain a competitive edge, and foster long-term growth.

Techniques to foster creativity

1. Brainstorming

Definition and Purpose

- **Brainstorming** in a business setting involves generating a wide range of ideas or solutions to address specific challenges, develop new products, or enhance processes. The goal is to leverage collective creativity and diverse perspectives to explore multiple possibilities. Brainstorming is a creative process designed to generate a large number of ideas in a short period. It encourages open and spontaneous thinking to solve problems, develop new concepts, or enhance existing processes. The key principle is to suspend judgment and focus on idea generation.

Applications in Business

1. Product Development

- **Idea Generation**: Brainstorming sessions are used to develop new product concepts, features, or enhancements. Teams generate a wide range of ideas, from incremental improvements to revolutionary innovations.
- **Feature Prioritization**: After generating ideas, brainstorming helps in identifying which features or concepts are most promising and worth pursuing.

2. Marketing Strategies

- **Campaign Ideas**: Marketing teams use brainstorming to come up with creative campaign ideas, branding strategies, and promotional tactics. This process helps in identifying unique angles and approaches to engage target audiences.
- **Content Creation**: Brainstorming can also be used to generate content ideas for blogs, social media, and other marketing channels, ensuring a steady flow of fresh and relevant material.

3. Problem Solving

- **Operational Challenges**: When faced with operational issues or inefficiencies, brainstorming sessions help in exploring various solutions and approaches. This can lead to innovative strategies for overcoming obstacles.
- **Strategic Planning**: Teams brainstorm to address strategic challenges, such as market entry, competitive positioning, or organizational change. This helps in developing diverse strategies and identifying potential risks

and opportunities.

4. Organizational Development

- **Process Improvement:** Brainstorming is used to identify ways to streamline operations, enhance productivity, and improve internal processes. This can lead to more efficient workflows and better resource utilization.
- **Employee Engagement:** Engaging employees in brainstorming sessions can boost morale and foster a sense of involvement in decision-making, leading to higher job satisfaction and productivity.

Best Practices for Effective Brainstorming

1. Set Clear Objectives

- **Define the Problem:** Clearly define the problem or challenge that needs to be addressed. This ensures that the brainstorming session stays focused and productive.
- **Establish Goals:** Set specific goals for the session, such as generating a certain number of ideas or exploring particular aspects of the problem.

2. Create a Conducive Environment

- **Encourage Open Communication:** Foster an open and supportive environment where participants feel comfortable sharing their ideas without fear of criticism.
- **Provide Resources:** Use tools like whiteboards, sticky notes, or digital collaboration platforms to capture and organize ideas effectively.

3. Encourage Diverse Participation

- **Include Various Perspectives:** Involve team members from different departments, backgrounds, and expertise areas to bring diverse viewpoints and ideas.
- **Promote Inclusivity:** Ensure that all participants have an opportunity to contribute and that quieter voices are heard.

4. Focus on Quantity First

- **Generate a High Volume of Ideas**: Emphasize the generation of a large number of ideas, without worrying about feasibility or quality initially. This can lead to unexpected and innovative solutions.
- **Build on Ideas**: Encourage participants to build on each other's ideas and combine them to create new and improved concepts.

5. Avoid Immediate Criticism

- **Suspend Judgment**: Refrain from evaluating or criticizing ideas during the brainstorming phase. This allows for a free flow of creativity and prevents participants from self-censoring.
- **Focus on Ideation**: Separate the idea generation phase from the evaluation phase to ensure a productive and creative process.

6. Organize and Evaluate Ideas

- **Categorize Ideas**: After the brainstorming session, categorize and group similar ideas to identify common themes and trends.
- **Prioritize and Refine**: Evaluate and prioritize the ideas based on criteria such as feasibility, impact, and alignment with business goals. Refine and develop the most promising ideas further.

How Brainstorming Fosters Creativity

1. Encourages Divergent Thinking

Divergent thinking is the ability to generate a wide range of ideas and solutions. Brainstorming promotes this by encouraging participants to think freely and explore various possibilities.In brainstorming sessions, there is no immediate critique of ideas, allowing participants to explore creative and unconventional solutions without self-censorship. This freedom leads to a broader array of ideas, some of which might be innovative or unorthodox.

2. Leverages Collective Intelligence

Collective intelligence refers to the combined knowledge and creativity of a group. Brainstorming taps into the diverse experiences and perspectives of team members.By involving individuals from different departments, backgrounds, and expertise areas, brainstorming sessions can generate a richer pool of ideas. This diversity can lead to more comprehensive and innovative solutions that might not emerge from individual thinking alone.

3. Breaks Down Mental Barriers

Mental barriers are constraints that limit creative thinking, such as fear of judgment or adherence to conventional approaches. Brainstorming helps break down these barriers. Creating an open and non-judgmental environment encourages participants to express their ideas freely. This can lead to the discovery of novel solutions and new ways of approaching problems, as participants are less likely to be constrained by traditional thinking.

4. Stimulates Idea Generation

Idea generation is the process of producing new concepts or solutions. Brainstorming actively stimulates this process by providing a structured approach to idea generation.Techniques like free association, mind mapping, and role playing within brainstorming sessions can spark new ideas. For example, using prompts or challenges can stimulate participants to think creatively and generate a higher volume of ideas.

5. Facilitates Collaboration and Teamwork

Collaboration involves working together to achieve a common goal. Brainstorming sessions inherently foster collaboration and teamwork. Brainstorming brings team members together, encouraging them to share their ideas and build on each other's contributions. This collaborative environment can lead to the development of more refined and effective solutions, as team members combine their insights and expertise.

6. Promotes Open Communication

Open communication involves the free exchange of ideas and information. Brainstorming creates a space where open communication is encouraged. By establishing a safe and supportive atmosphere, brainstorming sessions promote open dialogue. Participants feel more comfortable sharing their ideas, which can lead to a more thorough exploration of potential solutions and a deeper understanding of the problem at hand.

2. Role Playing

Definition and Purpose

- **Role Playing** involves acting out scenarios or assuming different roles to explore various perspectives and test ideas in a simulated environment. In business, it's used to understand stakeholder viewpoints, test strategies, and enhance decision-making.

Applications in Business

1. Product and Service Design

- **Customer Perspective**: Teams role play as customers to understand their needs, preferences, and pain points. By simulating the customer experience, businesses can identify areas for improvement, innovate new features, and create products or services that better meet customer expectations.
- **Service Scenarios**: Role playing can help design and refine customer service interactions. By acting out customer service scenarios, businesses can develop more effective communication strategies, identify common issues, and enhance overall service quality.

2. Marketing and Sales

- **Campaign Testing**: Role playing can be used to test marketing messages and sales pitches. Participants act as potential customers or clients to provide feedback on the effectiveness of different promotional approaches and identify areas for improvement.
- **Sales Training**: Sales teams can use role playing to practice and refine their sales techniques. By simulating real-life sales situations, team members can improve their persuasion skills, handle objections more effectively, and build stronger customer relationships.

3. Problem-Solving and Strategy Development

- **Scenario Analysis**: Role playing allows teams to simulate various business scenarios, such as market changes, competitive threats, or crisis situations. This helps in developing and testing strategic responses, identifying potential challenges, and preparing for unforeseen events.

- **Strategic Planning**: By assuming different roles, such as those of competitors or stakeholders, teams can gain insights into how different strategies might play out and refine their plans accordingly.

4. Team Building and Collaboration

- **Understanding Perspectives**: Role playing helps team members understand and appreciate each other's viewpoints. This fosters empathy, enhances communication, and strengthens teamwork by highlighting how different roles contribute to the overall objectives.
- **Conflict Resolution**: Role playing can be used to address and resolve interpersonal conflicts within teams. By acting out conflicts and their resolutions, team members can develop better conflict management skills and find mutually agreeable solutions.

Benefits of Role Playing

1. Enhanced Empathy

- **Understanding Stakeholders**: Role playing helps participants step into the shoes of different stakeholders, such as customers, clients, or team members. This deepens their understanding of others' needs, challenges, and perspectives, leading to more empathetic and customer-focused solutions.

2. Practical Insights

- **Real-World Application**: By simulating real-life scenarios, role playing provides practical insights into how different ideas and strategies might work in practice. This can lead to more realistic and actionable solutions.

3. Improved Creativity

- **Exploring Possibilities**: Role playing encourages participants to think creatively and explore various possibilities. It opens up new ways of thinking by presenting scenarios that may not be considered in traditional brainstorming sessions.

4. Skill Development

- **Communication and Negotiation**: Role playing helps participants develop essential skills such as communication, negotiation, and problem-solving. These skills are critical for effective collaboration and successful business interactions.

Best Practices for Role Playing

1. Design Relevant Scenarios

- **Realistic and Relevant**: Ensure that the scenarios used in role playing are realistic and relevant to the business context. This ensures that the insights gained are applicable and valuable.

2. Define Clear Roles

- **Role Clarity**: Clearly define the roles that participants will assume and provide background information on each role. This helps participants understand their perspectives and engage more effectively in the simulation.

3. Facilitate Debriefing

- **Discussion and Reflection**: After the role playing session, conduct a debriefing to discuss observations, insights, and potential improvements. This helps in translating the experience into actionable strategies and solutions.

4. Encourage Participation

- **Inclusive Environment**: Create a supportive environment where all participants feel comfortable sharing their ideas and experiences. Encourage active participation and feedback from everyone involved.

5. Iterate and Refine

- **Continuous Improvement**: Use role playing as an iterative process. Continuously refine scenarios, roles, and approaches based on feedback and insights to enhance the effectiveness of the technique.

3.Incubation

Incubation is a creativity technique that involves taking a break from actively thinking about a problem or idea, allowing the subconscious mind to process information. This process often leads to creative insights or solutions emerging when you return to the problem.

How Incubation Works:

1. Initial Engagement:

- Begin with an intense focus on the problem. This phase involves deep thinking, brainstorming, research, or problem-solving attempts. It's crucial to immerse yourself fully in the issue to load your mind with relevant information and context.

2. Detachment:

- After a period of focused work, step away from the problem. This detachment can take various forms, such as engaging in unrelated activities, exercising, sleeping, or simply relaxing. The idea is to let go of conscious thought about the problem.

3. Subconscious Processing:

- During this break, your subconscious mind continues to work on the problem. Without the constraints of focused thought, the brain is free to make connections between seemingly unrelated pieces of information, leading to novel ideas or solutions.

4. *Insight:*

- Upon returning to the problem, you may experience a sudden insight or "Aha moment," where a solution or creative idea that was previously out of reach becomes clear. This is the result of the subconscious processing that occurred during the incubation period.

Application in Business:

- **Problem-Solving**: Use incubation when you're stuck on a difficult problem. After gathering all the necessary information and analyzing it, take a break and let your subconscious do the work.
- **Creative Projects**: Incorporate incubation periods into project timelines, allowing ideas to mature and develop naturally over time.
- **Decision-Making**: When faced with a critical decision, give yourself some time away from the issue before finalizing your choice, which might lead to more creative solutions.

Benefits of Incubation:

- **Reduced Mental Fatigue**: Stepping away from a problem can reduce stress and prevent mental fatigue, which often blocks creativity.
- **Increased Creativity**: Incubation allows for the unconscious combination of ideas, leading to innovative solutions.
- **Improved Problem Solving**: By allowing the mind to explore solutions subconsciously, incubation can lead to more effective and creative problem-solving outcomes.

Creativity Tools and Technique

SCAMPER

- SCAMPER is a creative thinking technique designed to help people generate ideas or improve existing ones by systematically exploring different aspects of a product, service, or process. The acronym SCAMPER stands for Substitute, Combine, Adapt, Modify, Put to another use, Eliminate, and Rearrange/Reverse. Each element of SCAMPER encourages users to think about the problem or challenge from a different perspective.

SCAMPER Breakdown:

Substitute:

Think about what you can substitute in your product, service, or process. What materials, components, or resources can be replaced? Can you substitute one method for another?Example: Replacing plastic packaging with biodegradable materials.

Combine:

Explore how you can combine two or more elements to create something new. Can you combine different products, services, or processes? What if you merge two functions or ideas?Example: Combining a smartphone with a camera to create a smartphone with advanced photography capabilities.

Adapt:

Think about how you can adapt your idea to new contexts or situations. How can you modify the product for a different use? Can it be adjusted to serve a new market?Example: Adapting a fitness app for use in physical therapy.

Modify:

Consider ways to modify your product, service, or process.What can you change in terms of size, shape, color, or functionality? How can you enhance the value?Example: Redesigning a car to be more compact and fuel-efficient.

Put to Another Use:

Find new uses for your product or service. How else can this be used? Can it be applied in a different industry?Example: Using drones originally designed for military purposes in agriculture for crop monitoring.

Eliminate:

Think about what you can eliminate to simplify the product or process. What elements can be removed without affecting functionality? Can you reduce waste or unnecessary steps?Example: Removing excess packaging to reduce environmental impact.

Rearrange/Reverse:

Consider rearranging the order or reversing the process. What happens if you reverse the sequence? Can you reorder the steps to improve efficiency?Rearranging the customer service process to provide support before the sale rather than after.

Application of SCAMPER in Business:

- Product Development: SCAMPER can be used to innovate new products or improve existing ones by systematically questioning and altering various aspects of the product.

- Process Improvement: Businesses can apply SCAMPER to streamline processes, reduce costs, and improve efficiency.
- Marketing Strategies: SCAMPER can help generate fresh ideas for marketing campaigns, advertising, and customer engagement by altering elements of the message, medium, or audience.
-

Benefits of SCAMPER:

- Structured Creativity: SCAMPER provides a systematic approach to creativity, making it easier to generate and evaluate ideas.
- Versatility: It can be applied to any aspect of a business, from product development to operations to marketing.
- Comprehensive Exploration: By examining multiple facets of a problem or idea, SCAMPER encourages a thorough exploration of possibilities.

Mind Mapping

Mind Mapping is a visual tool used to organize and represent ideas, concepts, and information. It allows for the brainstorming, structuring, and exploration of relationships between different ideas in a non-linear way. Mind maps are particularly useful for both individual and group settings, helping to foster creativity and enhance problem-solving capabilities. Mind mapping is defined as a versatile tool that can significantly enhance creativity in business by visually organizing ideas, concepts, and strategies. It starts with a central idea and branches out to show related thoughts, tasks, and information. This method uses words and images, making it more engaging than traditional note-taking.

How Mind Mapping Works:

- **Central Idea**:
  - Begin with a central idea or problem in the middle of a blank page or digital canvas. This serves as the starting point for the mind map.

- **Main Branches:**
    - Draw branches radiating out from the central idea. Each branch represents a key theme, category, or component related to the central idea.
- **Sub-Branches:**
    - From each main branch, draw sub-branches that break down the main themes into more specific ideas, details, or subcategories. This creates a hierarchical structure that visually organizes the information.
- **Visual Elements:**
    - Enhance the mind map with colors, images, symbols, and keywords to make it more engaging and easier to understand. Visual elements not only make the mind map more appealing but also help in memory retention.
- **Continuous Expansion:**
    - Mind maps are flexible and can be continuously expanded as new ideas or information emerges. This makes them ideal for dynamic brainstorming sessions or ongoing project planning.

Application of Mind Mapping in Business:

- **Brainstorming:** Use mind maps to capture and organize ideas during brainstorming sessions, helping teams visualize connections between concepts and encouraging free-thinking.
- **Strategic Planning:** Mind maps can be used to outline strategic plans, breaking down goals, strategies, and action steps into a clear, visual format.
- **Project Management:** Create mind maps to outline project tasks, timelines, and responsibilities, ensuring that all aspects of the project are

considered and managed effectively.

- **Problem-Solving**: Mind maps can help explore different solutions to a problem by visually mapping out various options, potential outcomes, and their interrelationships.

Benefits of Mind Mapping:

Enhanced Creativity: The non-linear format of mind mapping encourages the exploration of diverse ideas and helps generate creative solutions.

Improved Organization: Mind maps help organize complex information in a visually clear and accessible way, making it easier to understand and communicate.

Better Memory and Retention: We've all forgotten a great idea at some point, and that can be a big problem when you're working on a project or trying to build your business strategy. Mind mapping gives you a chance to focus on new ideas without losing the old ones because you've got all your thoughts organized in one place.Staying organized is always so important when you're running a business, and using mind maps can be a great way to keep track of new ideas. The use of colors, images, and spatial organization in mind mapping enhances memory and recall, making it a powerful tool for learning and knowledge retention.

Improves team Collaboration: Mind maps are particularly effective in collaborative settings, allowing teams to build on each other's ideas and create a shared vision of the project or problem.Mind maps are great because several people can work together to brainstorm ideas, and those same people can work together to figure out how to transform those ideas into actions. When everyone has input, it's a lot easier to get your team to collaborate.

Boosts productivity: Creating mind maps can help boost productivity by keeping the team focused on a central idea. Whether you're brainstorming ideas for a project or working on your branding or business strategy, mind maps allow everyone to come together and focus on one thing. Unlike traditional linear note-taking, mind maps are short and to the point, so mind mapping can save you time over other types of brainstorming and strategizing.

Improves critical thinking: Whether you're building your digital brand or figuring out how to tackle a project, critical thinking is a lot easier with concept maps. Mind maps give people a chance to write down all of their important ideas without fleshing them out fully. You don't have to write out lengthy paragraphs or attach detailed notes to every word or phrase, which means you can focus more of your energy on critical thinking. Mind maps are also helpful because the whole team can collaborate to turn critical thinking into actionable ideas.

CHAPTER TWO

INNOVATION AND ITS ROLE IN BUSINESS

In the business world, innovation is not just about creating something new; it's about generating value in ways that were previously unimaginable. Whether through the development of groundbreaking products, the refinement of processes, or the reinvention of business models, innovation is a powerful force that enables companies to adapt, grow, and lead in an ever-changing landscape. It is the key to staying relevant in a competitive marketplace, meeting the evolving needs of customers, and addressing the complex challenges of our time. As technology advances and global markets expand, the demand for innovation has never been greater. Embracing innovation means fostering a culture of creativity, risk-taking, and continuous improvement, ensuring that businesses are not just participants in the future but architects of it.The term **"innovation"** finds its origins in the Latin verb Innovare, signifying renewal. Innovation is defined as the process of bringing about new ideas, methods, products, services, or solutions that have a significant positive impact and value. It involves transforming creative concepts into tangible outcomes that improve efficiency, and effectiveness, or address unmet needs

Business innovation is defined as the process of creating and implementing new ideas, methods, products, or services within an organization to improve its sales performance, competitiveness, and value creation of customers. Innovation is a product, service, business model, or strategy that's both novel and useful. Innovations don't have to be major breakthroughs in technology or new business models; they can be as simple as upgrades to a company's customer service or features added to an existing product. Innovation involves a continuous and adaptive journey, requiring organizations to foster a culture that encourages creativity, embraces change, and pursues solutions that lead to meaningful advancements. Innovation is vital for businesses to remain competitive, adapt to changing environments, and create value for customers and stakeholders. By fostering a culture of innovation, businesses can continuously evolve and thrive in the face of challenges and opportunities. it involves thinking differently, challenging the status quo, and implementing changes that can lead to significant improvements or entirely new offerings.

Innovation differs from invention, Invention refers to the creation of something entirely new, innovation involves the effective application and implementation of inventive ideas to generate practical and impactful outcomes, driving continuous improvement and positive change in the dynamic landscapes of business, technology, and society.

Some of the examples of business innovations

- **Apple:** Revolutionized the tech industry with product innovations like the iPhone, iPad, and MacBook, coupled with a robust ecosystem of services.
- **Tesla:** Disrupted the automotive industry with electric vehicles, battery technology, and autonomous driving innovations.
- **Amazon:** Innovated in retail with e-commerce, cloud computing (AWS), and logistics, redefining customer expectations for speed and convenience.
- **Netflix:** Transformed the entertainment industry by shifting from DVD rentals to a streaming service model and investing in original content.

Types of innovation

Innovation can take many forms, depending on the area of application, the approach taken, and the desired outcome. Here are detailed notes on the different types of innovation:

1. *Product Innovation*

Product innovation involves the development of new products or significant improvements to existing products. This type of innovation focuses on enhancing the features, functionality, design, or performance of a product to better meet customer needs or open up new market opportunities. By introducing new or upgraded products, companies can increase market share by attracting new customers, enhance customer satisfaction and loyalty with improved solutions, and drive revenue growth

Some of the Examples are :

- **New Product Development**: Introducing a completely new product to the market, such as the first smartphone or electric vehicle.
- **Product Improvement**: Enhancing an existing product, such as adding a new feature to a software application or improving the battery life of a mobile device.
- **Product Line Expansion**: Expanding a product line by adding new variations or versions of existing products, such as launching a new flavor of a popular snack.

2. Process Innovation

Process innovation involves changes to the methods, techniques, or systems used in producing or delivering products and services. It focuses on improving efficiency, reducing costs, and enhancing the quality of the output. It results low production costs and increases profitability, improves product quality and consistency, and enhances the speed and efficiency of service delivery.

Examples are

- **Automation**: Implementing robotics or AI to automate manufacturing processes, reducing human error and increasing production speed.
- **Lean Manufacturing**: Adopting lean principles to eliminate waste and optimize resource use in production.
- **Supply Chain Optimization**: Improving supply chain logistics to reduce lead times and minimize inventory costs.

3. Business Model Innovation

Business model innovation involves changing the way a company creates, delivers, and captures value. This type of innovation can redefine the company's core activities, revenue streams, customer relationships, and value propositions. This innovation opens up new revenue streams and market segments, enhances customer retention through recurring revenue models, and disrupts traditional industries by offering innovative value propositions, driving significant competitive advantage and long-term growth.

Examples:

- **Subscription-Based Model:** Transitioning from a one-time purchase model to a subscription-based model, as seen with software companies like Adobe and Microsoft.
- **Freemium Model:** Offering a basic product or service for free while charging for premium features, commonly used by digital platforms like Spotify or LinkedIn.
- **Platform-Based Model:** Creating a platform that connects buyers and sellers, as seen with e-commerce giants like Amazon or ride-sharing services like Uber.

4. Service Innovation

Service innovation involves the development of new or improved services that better meet the needs of customers. This can include changes to how services are delivered, the introduction of new service offerings, or enhancements to the customer experience. Service innovation increases customer satisfaction by providing more convenient and tailored services, reduces operational costs by automating service delivery, and strengthens customer loyalty through enhanced service quality.

Examples:

- **Personalized Services:** Offering customized services based on customer preferences, such as personalized streaming recommendations on Netflix.

- **Self-Service Options**: Implementing self-service kiosks in retail or digital platforms for banking, allowing customers to complete transactions independently.
- **Omnichannel Experience**: Providing a seamless customer experience across multiple channels, such as online, in-store, and via mobile apps.

5. Organizational Innovation

Organizational innovation refers to changes in a company's structure, management practices, or internal processes that improve efficiency, productivity, and employee satisfaction. It focuses on how the organization is structured and how it operates. Organizational innovation enhances agility and responsiveness to change, improves employee engagement and retention by fostering a more dynamic work environment, and increases efficiency while reducing costs through streamlined processes.

Examples:

- **Agile Methodology**: Implementing agile practices to increase flexibility and responsiveness in project management and product development.
- **Flat Organizational Structure**: Reducing hierarchical levels to promote faster decision-making and empower employees.
- **Remote Work Policies**: Adopting remote work models to increase employee flexibility and reduce overhead costs.

6. Marketing Innovation

Marketing innovation involves the development of new strategies or approaches to promoting products and services. It focuses on how a company communicates with customers, builds brand awareness, and drives sales. Marketing innovation boosts brand visibility and engagement through creative techniques, strengthens customer relationships by delivering value beyond the product, and drives sales growth by reaching new customer segments and improving brand perception.

Examples:

- **Influencer Marketing**: Leveraging social media influencers to reach targeted audiences and build brand credibility.
- **Content Marketing**: Creating valuable content to attract and engage customers, such as blogs, videos, and webinars.
- **Experiential Marketing**: Offering immersive experiences, such as pop-up events or virtual reality demos, to create memorable customer interactions.

7. Technological Innovation

Technological innovation involves the development or application of new technologies to create or improve products, services, or processes. It is often a key driver of other types of innovation, as it enables new possibilities and efficiencies. Technological innovation drives significant impact by enabling companies to develop cutting-edge products and services, improving operational efficiency through automation and advanced tools, and creating new opportunities for market expansion and competitive advantage. It also enhances customer experiences by offering more personalized and efficient solutions, while facilitating faster and more accurate decision-making through data-driven insights.

Examples:

- **Artificial Intelligence (AI)**: Implementing AI to enhance decision-making, automate processes, or personalize customer experiences.
- **Blockchain**: Using blockchain technology for secure, transparent transactions in industries like finance, supply chain, and healthcare.
- **Internet of Things (IoT)**: Integrating IoT devices to monitor and optimize operations in real-time, such as smart home devices or industrial sensors.

8. Social Innovation

Social innovation refers to new strategies, concepts, and ideas that meet social needs and create new social relationships or collaborations. It focuses on improving the well-being of individuals and communities through innovative approaches. Social innovation addresses social challenges and improves the quality of life for individuals and communities, encourages collaboration between businesses, governments, and non-profits to create systemic change, and builds stronger, more resilient societies by fostering inclusive growth and development.

Examples:

- **Microfinance:** Providing small loans to individuals in low-income communities to promote entrepreneurship and economic development.
- **Social Enterprises:** Businesses that prioritize social impact alongside financial returns, such as companies focused on sustainable products or services that address social challenges.
- **Community Development Programs:** Initiatives that engage local communities in creating solutions to social issues, such as education, healthcare, or environmental sustainability.

9. Incremental Innovation

Incremental innovation involves making small, continuous improvements to existing products, services, or processes. It focuses on refining and optimizing what already exists rather than creating something entirely new. Incremental innovation helps maintain a competitive edge by continually updating products and services, ensuring they stay relevant. It enhances customer satisfaction through regular improvements in user experience and boosts efficiency while reducing costs through ongoing process optimization.

Examples:

- **Product Upgrades:** Regularly releasing new versions of a product with minor enhancements, such as software updates or new features in smartphones.
- **Process Improvements:** Continuously refining manufacturing processes to increase efficiency or reduce waste.
- **Customer Experience Enhancements:** Making small improvements to the customer service process, such as reducing wait times or simplifying the user interface of a website.

10. Disruptive Innovation

Disruptive innovation refers to the introduction of a product or service that significantly alters the market or industry. It often starts in niche markets but eventually displaces established competitors by offering a more accessible, affordable, or simpler solution. Disruptive innovation creates entirely new markets or significantly transforms existing ones, compelling established companies to adapt or face obsolescence. It frequently leads to widespread industry changes and the development of new business models.

Examples:

- **Digital Photography**: The shift from film to digital cameras disrupted the photography industry by making photography more accessible and convenient.
- **Streaming Services:** Services like Netflix disrupted the traditional television and movie rental industries by offering on-demand content via the internet.
- **Ride-Sharing**: Companies like Uber and Lyft disrupted the traditional taxi industry by providing more convenient and often cheaper alternatives through mobile apps.

11. Radical Innovation

Radical innovation involves the development of breakthrough technologies or products that create entirely new industries or drastically change existing ones. It represents a significant departure from existing practices or technologies. Radical change can lead to the creation of entirely new industries and redefine existing ones. It often demands significant investment in research and development and has the potential to generate substantial economic and social impact.

Examples:

- **The Internet**: The development of the internet revolutionized communication, commerce, and access to information, creating entirely new industries.
- **The Airplane:** The invention of the airplane transformed transportation and made global travel possible.

- **The Personal Computer**: The introduction of personal computers radically changed how people work, learn, and interact with technology.

12. Architectural Innovation

Architectural innovation involves reconfiguring the components of a product or system in a way that creates new interactions and capabilities. It changes the way different components or subsystems work together, rather than changing the components themselves. Architectural innovation creates new value propositions by rethinking how components interact, opens up new market opportunities with more flexible or customizable solutions, and often drives innovation at both the product and system levels

Examples:

- **Modular Smartphones**: Phones that allow users to swap out components like the camera or battery, changing the overall architecture of the device.
- **Hybrid Vehicles**: Combining traditional internal combustion engines with electric powertrains to create a new type of vehicle architecture.
- **Smart Home Systems**: Integrating various home devices, such as lighting, heating, and security, into a unified, interconnected system.

Innovation and creativity:

Creativity and innovation are important in business because each contributes to a dynamic evolution that prevents companies from stagnating and enables them to stay competitive in an ever-changing marketplace. While they are not the same, creativity can lead to innovation, so understanding each as two sides of the same coin is critical for business leaders.

Developing creativity and innovation in your organization means granting employees permission to try new approaches within the context of their current roles. This starts with company leadership and buy-in for attempting new things.

While these terms are often used interchangeably, they represent different stages in the journey from idea to impact. Creativity is generation of new and original ideas but innovation is implementation and application of ideas to create value. Creativity is often seen as the first step in the process, while innovation is the follow-through that brings those ideas to fruition. Creativity can be more abstract and conceptual, while innovation is practical and goal-oriented. Innovation is the action of putting things into practical reality, despite challenges and resistance, rather than just contemplating. It takes creative thinking, planning and implementation of new ideas to constitute innovation.

Relationship Between Creativity and Innovation – Differences

1. *Definition:*

    - Creativity: Creativity is the ability to generate new and original ideas, concepts, or solutions. It is the mental process of thinking outside the box, imagining possibilities, and coming up with unique approaches to problems.
    - Innovation: Innovation is the process of implementing those creative ideas into practical, tangible outcomes. It involves transforming creative concepts into products, services, processes, or methods that add value or bring about change.

2. *Nature:*

    - Creativity: It is primarily conceptual and abstract. Creativity is often unstructured and may not have immediate practical applications.
    - Innovation: Innovation is more practical and structured. It focuses on applying creative ideas in a real-world context to achieve a specific purpose or solve a particular problem.

3.

Process:

- Creativity: Creativity is about ideation, the generation of multiple potential ideas or solutions. It is often exploratory and speculative.
- Innovation: Innovation involves selection, development, and implementation of the most viable creative ideas. It requires planning, testing, and refining to ensure the idea can be effectively executed.

4.
Outcome:

- Creativity: The outcome of creativity is typically a novel idea or concept, which might be theoretical or impractical without further development.
- Innovation: The outcome of innovation is a practical product, service, or process that has been successfully brought to market or implemented within an organization.

5.
Measurement:

- Creativity: Creativity is difficult to measure quantitatively. It is often assessed qualitatively through originality, flexibility, and fluency of ideas.
- Innovation: Innovation can be measured more easily, often through metrics like revenue generation, market share, process improvement, or customer satisfaction.

6.
Risk:

- Creativity: Creativity carries lower immediate risk since it involves ideation without the commitment to implementation. However, the ideas may not always be feasible.

- Innovation: Innovation involves higher risk as it requires investment in time, resources, and money to turn ideas into reality. It also bears the risk of failure if the innovation doesn't achieve the desired outcomes.

7.

Skills Required:

- Creativity: Skills such as imagination, brainstorming, and divergent thinking are essential for creativity.
- Innovation: Innovation requires not only creative skills but also strategic planning, project management, and the ability to execute and commercialize ideas.

8.

Dependency:

- Creativity: Creativity can exist independently without necessarily leading to innovation.
- Innovation: Innovation depends on creativity as the starting point. Without creative ideas, innovation cannot occur.

Relationship Between Creativity and Innovation – Similarities

1.

Interconnection:

- Both creativity and innovation are closely linked and often interdependent. Creativity is the foundation for innovation, as innovative solutions or products originate from creative ideas. Without creativity, there can be no innovation, and innovation is the vehicle through which creative ideas are realized and brought to life.

2. ***Value Creation:***

   - Both creativity and innovation are aimed at adding value. Creativity adds value by bringing new ideas and perspectives, while innovation adds value by transforming these ideas into practical applications that benefit individuals, organizations, or society as a whole.

3. ***Problem-Solving:***

   - Both are essential for effective problem-solving. Creativity helps in generating multiple solutions or approaches to a problem, while innovation involves choosing the best solution and implementing it effectively to resolve the issue.

4. ***Involvement in Change:***

   - Both creativity and innovation are drivers of change. Creativity challenges the status quo by thinking differently, while innovation leads to actual change by implementing creative ideas in a way that alters existing processes, products, or services.

5. ***Fostering a Culture:***

   - Both creativity and innovation thrive in environments that encourage experimentation, risk-taking, and openness to new ideas. Organizations that foster a culture of creativity and innovation are often more adaptable and resilient in the face of change.

6. ***Skill Development:***

   - Both require the development of specific skills. Creativity involves skills such as imagination, lateral thinking, and open-mindedness. Innovation requires skills in project management, execution, and often cross-disciplinary knowledge. However, both also benefit from skills in collaboration and communication.

7. ***Role in Competitive Advantage:***

   - Both creativity and innovation contribute to an organization's competitive advantage. Creative thinking can lead to unique solutions that set an organization apart, while innovation turns these solutions into competitive products or services that offer differentiation in the marketplace.

8. ***Continuous Improvement:***

   - Both are essential for continuous improvement and growth. Creativity leads to new ideas for enhancing processes or products, while innovation ensures these ideas are tested, refined, and implemented to continually improve and stay relevant in the market.

Role of Innovation in Business Development

The importance of innovationin fostering competitive advantage, long-term sustainability, and organizational growth is pivotal. It propels businesses forward by differentiating them from competitors, reducing operational costs, and opening up new revenue streams. Moreover, innovation enhances customer satisfaction, attracts top talent, and ensures adaptability in the face of evolving market conditions. In essence, the importance of innovation extends beyond strategic choice; it is the heartbeat of thriving and resilient businesses in the modern world.Innovation is a critical driver of business development, encompassing various aspects of a company's operations, strategy, and long-term success. Below is a detailed exploration of how innovation influences and contributes to business development

1. Enhancing Competitive Advantage

- **Differentiation**: In highly competitive markets, innovation allows businesses to create unique products, services, or processes that distinguish them from competitors. This differentiation can be in the form of advanced technology, unique design, superior functionality, or exceptional customer service. A differentiated offering often leads to increased market share and customer loyalty, as consumers are drawn to something new and valuable.
- **Brand Reputation**: Companies known for their innovative capabilities often build a strong brand reputation. This reputation can attract new customers, retain existing ones, and even draw top talent to the organization. Being perceived as an industry leader in innovation can also lead to partnerships and opportunities that further bolster the company's market position.

2. Driving Growth and Expansion

- **Access to New Markets**: Innovation can be a key factor in entering new markets. By developing products or services that address unmet needs in different regions, demographics, or sectors, businesses can tap into new customer bases. For instance, a company might innovate by adapting its offerings to suit local tastes or by introducing new technologies that cater to specific market demands.
- **Creating New Revenue Streams**: Innovation often leads to the development of new products or services that can diversify a company's revenue streams. This diversification reduces reliance on a single product or market and spreads risk, contributing to financial stability and growth. For example, a tech company might innovate by offering a new software solution that complements its existing hardware products, thus creating an additional revenue source.

3. *Improving Efficiency and Reducing Costs*

- **Process Innovation**: Innovations in business processes, such as the adoption of automation, lean manufacturing techniques, or digital transformation, can significantly enhance operational efficiency. By streamlining processes, reducing waste, and minimizing errors, companies can lower production costs, increase output, and improve quality. This efficiency not only boosts profitability but also allows businesses to offer competitive pricing.
- **Optimizing Resource Utilization**: Innovation in resource management—such as the use of renewable energy, recycling of materials, or innovative supply chain practices—can lead to better utilization of resources. This optimization reduces costs and improves sustainability, which is increasingly important in today's business environment. Efficient resource use also helps companies respond more flexibly to changes in supply or demand.

4. *Meeting Customer Needs*

- **Developing Customer-Centric Solutions**: Innovation enables businesses to better understand and anticipate customer needs, leading to the creation of products and services that offer greater value. For example, through customer feedback and data analysis, a company might innovate by improving the user experience of its product, making it more intuitive and user-friendly. This focus on customer-centric innovation enhances customer satisfaction and loyalty.
- **Personalization and Customization**: Innovations in data analytics and artificial intelligence allow businesses to offer personalized experiences to customers. By tailoring products, services, and marketing messages to individual preferences, companies can increase customer engagement and build stronger relationships. Personalization is a powerful tool for differentiation and can lead to higher conversion rates and repeat business.

5. Adapting to Change

- **Responding to Market Dynamics**: Innovation is essential for businesses to adapt to changing market conditions, such as new regulations, economic shifts, or technological advancements. For instance, a company might innovate by adopting new technologies that reduce its carbon footprint in response to environmental regulations. By staying agile and responsive, businesses can maintain their competitive edge and avoid obsolescence.
- **Crisis Management and Resilience**: During economic downturns or crises, such as the COVID-19 pandemic, innovation can help businesses pivot their strategies and find new ways to sustain operations. For example, many companies innovated by transitioning to online platforms and remote work models during the pandemic, allowing them to continue serving customers despite lockdowns and restrictions.

6. Fostering a Culture of Continuous Improvement

- **Encouraging Creativity and Experimentation**: Innovation fosters a culture where creativity and experimentation are valued. This environment encourages employees to think outside the box, explore new ideas, and challenge the status quo. A culture of continuous improvement leads to ongoing innovation, as employees are motivated to find better ways to do things and to develop new products or services.
- **Enhancing Employee Engagement and Retention**: When employees are involved in the innovation process, they often feel more engaged and motivated. Innovation provides opportunities for professional growth and development, which can lead to higher job satisfaction and lower turnover rates. Companies that promote a culture of innovation are also more likely to attract and retain top talent.

7. Leveraging Technology for Business Transformation

- **Digital Transformation:** Innovation often involves the adoption of new technologies that can transform business models and operations. For example, the integration of artificial intelligence, big data analytics, or cloud computing can revolutionize how a business operates, making it more efficient, responsive, and scalable. Digital transformation enables companies to better serve customers, streamline processes, and innovate at a faster pace.
- **Data-Driven Decision-Making:** Technological innovations allow businesses to gather and analyze data more effectively. With advanced data analytics, companies can make informed decisions based on real-time insights, leading to better strategic planning and execution. Data-driven innovation helps businesses identify trends, predict customer behavior, and optimize operations.

8. *Ensuring Sustainability and Long-Term Viability*

- **Environmental and Social Innovation:** In today's business environment, sustainability is increasingly important. Innovations in eco-friendly products, green technologies, and sustainable business practices can help companies reduce their environmental impact and meet the growing demand for corporate social responsibility. For example, a company might innovate by developing a biodegradable product that reduces plastic waste, thereby appealing to environmentally conscious consumers.
- **Future-Proofing the Business:** Innovation helps businesses anticipate future trends and challenges, allowing them to adapt and remain viable in the long term. By investing in research and development, exploring emerging technologies, and staying ahead of industry trends, companies can future-proof their business and ensure long-term success.

9. *Creating Collaborative Opportunities*

- **Forming Strategic Partnerships and Alliances:** Innovation often leads to new partnerships with other companies, startups, or research institutions. These collaborations can enhance a company's capabilities, share risks, and accelerate growth. For example, a tech company might partner with a university to develop cutting-edge technology, benefiting from academic expertise and research facilities.

- **Open Innovation**: Open innovation involves sharing ideas, technologies, and resources across organizational boundaries to create new opportunities. By engaging in open innovation, companies can leverage external expertise, reduce development time, and increase the chances of success. This collaborative approach can lead to breakthrough innovations that drive business development.

10. Enhancing Customer Experience

- **Innovating in Service Delivery**: Innovations in service delivery can significantly improve the customer experience. For example, companies might use automation to speed up service, implement AI-powered chatbots for customer support, or develop mobile apps that provide customers with seamless access to services. These innovations enhance convenience, reliability, and overall customer satisfaction.
- **Utilizing Feedback Loops**: Innovative companies often establish feedback loops that allow them to continuously gather customer input and refine their offerings. By listening to customers and making iterative improvements, businesses can ensure their products and services remain relevant and meet evolving customer needs.

Barriers to Innovation

1. Organizational Culture

  - **Conservatism and Risk Aversion:** In some organizations, there is a deep-rooted culture of conservatism were sticking to proven methods is valued over experimentation. This risk-averse attitude can significantly hinder innovation as employees may feel discouraged from trying new approaches or suggesting creative ideas.

- **Lack of Collaboration**: Innovation often requires collaboration across different departments and functions. However, in organizations where silos (isolation)exist, communication and cooperation between teams can be limited, leading to isolated efforts that do not leverage the full potential of the organization.
- **Fear of Failure**: A culture that penalizes failure can stifle innovation. Employees may avoid taking risks if they fear that failure will lead to reprimand or job insecurity. This fear prevents the experimentation and iteration necessary for innovation.

This barrier creates some impact on the society. Employees may refrain from proposing innovative ideas, fearing they won't be supported or will be outright rejected. Another problem is **Stagnation**: Without a culture that supports innovation, the organization may stagnate, falling behind competitors who are more adaptive and forward-thinking.

2. Lack of Resources

- **Financial Constraints**: Innovation often requires investment in research and development, new technologies, and the recruitment of specialized talent. Organizations operating on tight budgets may prioritize short-term profitability over long-term innovation, leading to underfunded projects.
- **Human Resources**: A shortage of skilled personnel with the expertise needed to drive innovation can be a significant barrier. Additionally, existing staff may already be overburdened with routine tasks, leaving little time for innovative thinking.
- **Time Constraints**: Innovation requires time for experimentation, development, and refinement. Organizations focused on immediate results may not allocate sufficient time for innovation projects, leading to rushed or incomplete efforts.

Lack of funding, talent, and time can result in innovative ideas that are poorly executed or abandoned entirely. Companies may miss out on market opportunities or fall behind competitors due to their inability to invest in necessary resources.

3. Resistance to Change

- **Employee Resistance**: Employees may resist new technologies, processes, or ways of working due to comfort with existing routines, fear of job loss, or lack of confidence in their ability to adapt.
- **Managerial Resistance**: Managers may resist innovation initiatives that they perceive as risky or threatening to their control. They may also be reluctant to support changes that could disrupt current operations or challenge their authority.
- **Stakeholder Resistance**: Other stakeholders, such as customers, suppliers, or investors, may be resistant to changes if they believe it will negatively impact them. This can include concerns about product changes, shifts in business strategy, or alterations to established relationships.

These barriers create innovation blockage and slow adoption. Resistance can prevent innovative ideas from being fully explored or implemented, resulting in lost opportunities. Even when innovative ideas are accepted, resistance can slow down the adoption process, delaying the benefits of innovation.

4. Poor Leadership

- **Lack of Vision**: Leaders who lack a clear vision for the future may struggle to guide their organizations towards innovation. Without a strategic direction, innovation efforts may be unfocused or misaligned with the company's goals.
- **Inadequate Support**: Innovation requires strong support from leadership, including providing resources, removing obstacles, and fostering a culture that encourages creativity. Leaders who do not prioritize or champion innovation can demotivate employees and stifle innovation efforts.
- **Micromanagement**: Leaders who micromanage may inadvertently suppress innovation by not giving employees the autonomy they need to explore new ideas and take risks.

Demoralized Workforce is one of the impact of poor leadership.Poor leadership can lead to a lack of motivation and creativity among employees, reducing the overall innovative capacity of the organization. Without strong leadership, innovation efforts may become fragmented, leading to wasted resources and missed strategic opportunities.

5. Inadequate Communication

- **Lack of Clear Communication:** When there is insufficient communication about innovation goals, processes, or expectations, employees may be unclear about their role in innovation efforts. This can lead to confusion and a lack of alignment within the organization.
- **Information Silos:** In organizations where information is not shared freely across departments, employees may not have access to the knowledge and resources they need to innovate. This can result in duplicated efforts, missed opportunities for collaboration, and slower innovation progress.
- **Feedback Loops:** A lack of effective feedback mechanisms can hinder innovation by preventing the organization from learning from its successes and failures. Without feedback, it's difficult to refine and improve innovative ideas.

Misalignment and reduced collabrations are the Impact of this barrier.

Misalignment: Poor communication can lead to misaligned innovation efforts, where different parts of the organization are working towards conflicting or unclear goals.

Reduced Collaboration: Inadequate communication can prevent the sharing of ideas and resources across the organization, limiting the potential for cross-functional innovation.

6. Regulatory and Legal Barriers

- **Compliance Requirements:** Innovation in highly regulated industries (e.g., healthcare, finance) can be slowed by the need to comply with complex regulatory requirements. This can increase the time and cost of bringing new products or services to market.

- **Intellectual Property Issues**: Concerns about protecting intellectual property (IP) can stifle innovation, particularly in industries where copying or patent infringement is common. Companies may be hesitant to share ideas or collaborate with others if they fear losing control of their IP.
- **Bureaucratic Hurdles**: In some cases, internal or external bureaucratic processes can create obstacles to innovation, such as lengthy approval processes, excessive documentation, or restrictive policies.

Regulatory and legal barriers can delay the development and introduction of innovative products or services, reducing the company's ability to respond quickly to market opportunities. Compliance with regulations can add significant costs to innovation projects, making them less feasible, especially for smaller companies.

Ways to Overcome Barriers to Innovation

Innovation is essential for organizations to stay competitive and thrive in today's rapidly evolving market. However, the path to innovation is often fraught with challenges that can impede progress and stifle creativity. These barriers—ranging from rigid organizational cultures and resource constraints to resistance to change and regulatory hurdles—can prevent even the most forward-thinking ideas from taking flight. Overcoming these barriers is not just about finding quick fixes; it requires a strategic approach that addresses underlying issues and fosters an environment where innovation can flourish. By understanding these obstacles and implementing targeted solutions, organizations can unlock their full potential and drive sustained growth and success. The best way of solving problems always starts with being aware that they actually exist in the first place.You will only be able to overcome them if you know that they're there. A thorough evaluation of your innovation process can help you identify these issues.

1. Fostering a Culture of Innovation

- **Encourage Risk-Taking:** Create an environment where calculated risks are encouraged and failure is viewed as a learning opportunity. This can be achieved by recognizing and rewarding innovative efforts, even when they don't succeed.
- **Promote Collaboration:** Break down silos by encouraging cross-functional teams and open communication. This can involve regular innovation meetings, workshops, or collaboration platforms that bring together diverse perspectives.
- **Support Continuous Learning:** Foster a culture of continuous learning by providing employees with opportunities for training and development in new skills and technologies. Encourage employees to stay curious and explore new ideas.

A culture that supports innovation will empower employees to think creatively, collaborate effectively, and take ownership of innovation initiatives.

2. Allocating Resources Strategically

- **Invest in Innovation:** Allocate a dedicated budget for innovation projects, ensuring that resources are available for research, development, and experimentation. This can also include setting up an innovation fund or incubator within the organization to support promising ideas.
- **Hire and Retain Talent:** Invest in recruiting and retaining talent with the skills and mindset needed to drive innovation. This may involve offering competitive salaries, career development opportunities, and a work environment that supports creativity.
- **Time Management:** Allow employees the time and space to focus on innovation by freeing them from routine tasks or allocating specific time for innovation activities (e.g., "innovation days" or hackathons).

Adequate resources ensure that innovation projects have the financial, human, and temporal support needed to succeed, leading to more impactful outcomes.

3. Managing Change Effectively

- **Change Management Programs**: Implement formal change management programs to help employees understand and embrace innovation. This can include training, communication plans, and involvement in the change process to reduce fear and resistance.
- **Leadership by Example**: Leaders should model the change they wish to see by actively participating in innovation initiatives and showing openness to new ideas. This can help build trust and demonstrate the organization's commitment to innovation.
- **Engage Stakeholders**: Involve key stakeholders early in the innovation process to address their concerns and gain their buy-in. This can include customers, suppliers, and investors who may be affected by changes resulting from innovation.

Effective change management reduces resistance, increases buy-in, and accelerates the adoption of innovative practices within the organization.

4. Strengthening Leadership Support

- **Vision and Strategy**: Leaders should clearly articulate a vision for innovation that aligns with the organization's overall strategy. This vision should be communicated regularly to keep innovation top-of-mind for all employees.
- **Empowerment**: Leaders should empower employees by providing them with the autonomy to explore new ideas and make decisions related to innovation. This can include decentralizing decision-making and encouraging bottom-up innovation.
- **Champion Innovation**: Leaders should actively champion innovation by providing resources, removing obstacles, and celebrating successes. This can involve sponsoring innovation initiatives, participating in innovation events, and publicly recognizing innovative contributions.

Strong leadership support ensures that innovation is prioritized and integrated into the organization's strategic goals, leading to more cohesive and sustained innovation efforts.

5. Enhancing Communication

- **Transparent Communication**: Ensure that communication about innovation goals, processes, and expectations is clear and consistent across the organization. Regular updates, town hall meetings, and internal newsletters can help keep everyone informed and aligned.
- **Open Information Sharing**: Encourage the free flow of information across departments by creating platforms for collaboration and knowledge sharing. This can include internal social networks, shared databases, or regular cross-functional meetings.
- **Feedback Mechanisms**: Establish feedback loops to collect input from employees, customers, and other stakeholders. This can involve surveys, suggestion boxes, or regular check-ins to gather insights and refine innovation efforts.

Improved communication leads to better alignment, increased collaboration, and more effective innovation efforts across the organization.

6. Navigating Regulatory and Legal Challenges

- **Stay Informed**: Keep abreast of relevant regulations and legal developments that may impact innovation efforts. This can involve working with legal and compliance teams to understand the implications of new laws or changes in the regulatory environment.
- **Collaborate with Regulators**: Engage with regulators early in the innovation process to seek guidance and address potential concerns. This can help ensure that innovation efforts are compliant with regulations while still pushing the boundaries of what is possible.
- **Protect Intellectual Property**: Develop a robust intellectual property strategy to protect innovations. This can include filing patents, securing trademarks, and establishing clear agreements with partners and collaborators to safeguard intellectual property.

By proactively managing regulatory and legal challenges, organizations can innovate within the boundaries of the law, reducing risks and ensuring that their innovations are sustainable and protected.

CHAPTER THREE

INTRODUCTION TO ENTREPRENEURSHIP

Entrepreneurship

Entrepreneurship is a dynamic and transformative force that drives economic growth, fosters innovation, and creates opportunities. At its core, entrepreneurship involves identifying and pursuing new business opportunities, taking risks, and bringing innovative ideas to life. Entrepreneurs play a crucial role in shaping industries, solving societal challenges, and generating employment. By leveraging creativity, resourcefulness, and strategic thinking, entrepreneurs build successful ventures and contribute to the broader economic and social fabric. This introduction explores the fundamental concepts of entrepreneurship, the traits of successful entrepreneurs, and the impact of entrepreneurial activities on the global economy.

Entrepreneurship is the ability and readiness to develop, organize, and run a business enterprise, along with any of its uncertainties in order to make a profit. The most prominent example of entrepreneurship is the starting of new businesses. Entrepreneurship may be defined as the visualization and realization of new ideas by insightful individuals, who can use information and mobilize resources to implement their vision. Entrepreneurship is the ability (i.e., knowledge plus skills) of a person to translate ideas of commencing a business unit into reality by setting up a business on the ground to serve the needs of society and the nation, in the hope of profits.

In the words of Stevenson and others, “Entrepreneurship is the process of creating value by bringing together a unique package of resources to exploit an opportunity." According to A.H. Cole, "Entrepreneurship is the purposeful activities of an individual or a group of associated individuals undertaken to initiate, maintain or organize a profit-oriented business unit for the production or distribution of economic goods and services".

Wennekers and Thurik have probably provided the most elaborate and inclusive definition:

" *Entrepreneurship is the manifest ability and willingness of individuals, on their own, in teams, within and outside existing organizations to perceive and create new economic opportunities (new products, new production methods, new organizational schemes and new product-market combinations), and to introduce their ideas in the market, in the face of uncertainty and other obstacles, by making decisions on location, form and the use of resources and institutions*"

An entrepreneur is an individual who identifies, develops, and manages a business venture or idea, taking on financial, managerial, and operational risks in pursuit of profit and growth. Entrepreneurs are often characterized by their innovation, resourcefulness, and willingness to take risks to create and grow new businesses. They play a crucial role in driving economic development, introducing new products or services, and contributing to job creation.

Characteristics of Entrepreneurship:

Ability to take a risk- Starting any new venture involves a considerable amount of failure risk. Therefore, an entrepreneur needs to be courageous and able to evaluate and take risks, which is an essential part of being an entrepreneur.

Innovation- It should be highly innovative to generate new ideas, start a company and earn profits out of it. Change can be the launching of a new product that is new to the market or a process that does the same thing but in a more efficient and economical way.

Visionary and Leadership quality- To be successful, the entrepreneur should have a clear vision of his new venture. However, to turn the idea into reality, a lot of resources and employees are required. Here, leadership quality is paramount because leaders impart and guide their employees towards the right path of success.

Open-Minded- In a business, every circumstance can be an opportunity and used for the benefit of a company. For example, Paytm recognised the gravity of demonetization and acknowledged the need for online transactions would be more, so it utilised the situation and expanded massively during this time.

Flexible- An entrepreneur should be flexible and open to change according to the situation. To be on the top, a businessperson should be equipped to embrace change in a product and service, as and when needed.

Know your Product-A company owner should know the product offerings and also be aware of the latest trend in the market. It is essential to know if the available product or service meets the demands of the current market, or whether it is time to tweak it a little. Being able to be accountable and then alter as needed is a vital part of entrepreneurship.

Importance of Entrepreneurship:

Creation of Employment- Entrepreneurship generates employment. It provides an entry-level job, required for gaining experience and training for unskilled workers.

Innovation- It is the hub of innovation that provides new product ventures, markets, technology quality of goods, etc., and increase the standard of living of people.

Impact on Society and Community Development- A society becomes greater if the employment base is large and diversified. It brings about changes in society and promotes facilities like higher expenditure on education, better sanitation, fewer slums, a higher level of homeownership. Therefore, entrepreneurship assists the organisation towards a more stable and high quality of community life.

Increase Standard of Living- Entrepreneurship helps to improve the standard of living of a person by increasing the income. The standard of living means an increase in the consumption of various goods and services by a household for a particular period.

Supports research and development- New products and services need to be researched and tested before launching in the market. Therefore, an entrepreneur also dispenses finance for research and development with research institutions and universities. This promotes research, general construction, and development in the economy.

Types of entrepreneurship

Based on Risk

(a)Innovative Entrepreneurship

Entrepreneur comes up with new ideas and turns them into viable business and find new ways to market the products that make their business stand out from the crowd and sometimes create a new crowd. Examples are Steve Jobs and Bill Gates.

(b) Imitative Entrepreneurship implements current techniques from which they copy certain business ideas and improve upon them as to gain an upper hand in the market. Imitative entrepreneurship is characterized by the adoption of exogenously changing technologies. Examples are development of small shopping complexes and small car manufacturers.

(c) Fabian Entrepreneurship is concerned with such business organizations in which the individual owner does not take initiative in visualizing and implementing new ideas and innovation. Dealings are determined by customs, religion, trading and past practices. They are not too interested in taking risks or changes and they try to follow the beaten track created by their predecessors.

(d) Drone Entrepreneurship is concerned with such businesses in which owners are satisfied with the existing mode and speed of business activity and show no inclination in gaining market leadership. They refuse to make any modification in the existing production methods in spite of incurring recurring losses.

Based on type of Business

(a) Agricultural Entrepreneurship covers a wide spectrum of agricultural activities like cultivation, marketing of agricultural produce, irrigation, mechanization and agricultural technology.

(b) Manufacturing Entrepreneurship identifies needs of customers and then explores the resources and technology to be used to manufacture the products to satisfy those needs by converting raw materials into finished products.

(c) Trading Entrepreneurship procures finished products from manufacturers and sells these to customers either directly or through middlemen such as wholesalers, dealers, and retailers. These middlemen act as a link between the manufacturer and customer.

(d)Business Entrepreneur: He is an individual who discovers an idea to start a business and then builds a business to give birth to his idea.

(e) Corporate Entrepreneur: He is a person who demonstrates his innovative skill in organizing and managing a corporate undertaking

Based of motivation:

Entrepreneurs are of the following types:

1) Pure Entrepreneur: They believe in their own performance while undertaking business activities. They undertake business ventures for their personal satisfaction, status and ego. They are guided by the motive of profit. For example, Dhirubhai Ambani of Reliance Group.

2) Induced Entrepreneur: He is induced to take up an entrepreneurial activity with a view to avail some benefits from the government. These benefits are in the form of assistance, incentives, subsidies, concessions and infrastructures.

3) Motivated Entrepreneur: These entrepreneurs are motivated by the desire to make use of their technical and professional expertise and skills. They are motivated by the desire forself-fulfillment.

4) Spontaneous Entrepreneur: They are motivated by their desire for self-employment and to achieve or prove their excellence in job performance. They are natural entrepreneurs.

Based on stages of development:

They may be classified into;

1) First Generation Entrepreneur: He is one who starts an industrial unit by means of his own innovative ideas and skills. He is essentially an innovator. He is also called new entrepreneur.

2) Modern Entrepreneur: He is an entrepreneur who undertakes those ventures which suit the modern marketing needs.

3) Classical Entrepreneur: He is one who develops a self supporting venture for the satisfaction of customers' needs. He is a stereo type or traditional entrepreneur

Based on use of Technology

(a) Technical Entrepreneurship deals with establishing and running industry based on science and technology. They use innovative methods of production.

(b)Non-Technical Entrepreneurship is concerned with the use of alternative and imitative methods of marketing and distribution strategies to make their business survive and thrive in a competitive market.

(c) Professional Entrepreneur: He is an entrepreneur who starts a business unit but does not carry on the business for long period. He sells out the running business and starts another venture

Based on Ownership

(a) Corporate entrepreneurship was pioneered by Burgelman. Corporate ownership is where an individual through innovation and skill organises, manages and controls a corporate undertaking efficiently.

(b) Private Entrepreneurship is where an individual sets up a business as a sole owner of the business and bears the entire risk involved in it.

(c) State Entrepreneurship is where trading or industrial venture is undertaken by the State or the Government.

(d) Joint Entrepreneurship implies a joint business endeavor between a private entrepreneur and the Government.

Based on size of Enterprise

1. Micro Enterprises: Any business with a turnover of up to Rupees five crore.

2. Small-Scale Entrepreneurship:A small enterprise has an annual turnover of more than Rupees five crore but not more than Rs 75 crore.

3. Medium-Scale Entrepreneurship: A business with a turnover over Rs 75 crore and upto Rs 250 crore

4. Large-Scale Entrepreneurship: Business with turnover over Rs 250 crore.

Based on Gender

Women Entrepreneurship

The Government of India defines women entrepreneurship as, "a business enterprise which is owned, managed and controlled by women having a minimum financial interest of 51 per cent of the capital and giving at least 51 per cent of employment generated in the enterprises to women." Schumpeter defines women entrepreneurship as, "based on women's participation in equity and employment of a business enterprise."

Based on Social Problems

Social Entrepreneurship

The concept of social entrepreneurship came around the 1960s but the establishment of Grameen Bank by Muhammad Yunus in Bangladesh was the first instance where it was thoroughly used. Social entrepreneurship focuses on social problems and environmental problems aiming at bringing about transformation. This obligation of contribution to social well-being is primary and in a way, profit takes a back seat or is more or less secondary but essential to the survival.

Intrapreneurship

Intrapreneurship refers to a system within a company or organization that allows employees to act like entrepreneurs. Intrapreneurs are self-motivated, proactive, and action-oriented individuals who take the initiative to develop innovative products or services.Unlike entrepreneurs, intrapreneurs operate within a company's safety net, absorbing any failures or losses. This support encourages creativity and risk-taking, allowing intrapreneurs to innovate without fearing personal financial loss. By leveraging their creativity and ingenuity, intrapreneurs can drive significant innovation and transform their workplaces, similar to entrepreneurs.

Who is an Intrapreneur

Intrapreneurs are employees of a company who are assigned to work on a special idea or project. They are given the time and freedom to develop the project as an entrepreneur would. However, they are not working solo. Intrapreneurs have the resources and capabilities of the firm at their disposal. An entrepreneur starts a company as a means of providing a good or service. An intrapreneur seeks to improve an existing company. Intrapreneurs and entrepreneurs have different objectives. An entrepreneur envisions creating a company from the ground up. An intrapreneur has a broader vision for an established company. This vision may involve radical changes to company traditions, processes, or products. The intrapreneur typically has direct applicable skills and experience to bring to the job.

An intrapreneur explores policies, technologies, or applications that will help improve the performance of an existing company. Inevitably, as an intrapreneur develops the skills needed to recognize and solve important problems, that intrapreneur may turn into an entrepreneur.

An intrapreneur can expect to be given the freedom and autonomy needed for such a project. Day-to-day deliverables are generally not demanded. The intrapreneur is expected to analyze and understand the trends necessary for planning the company's future. Intrapreneurs synthesize their findings and make proposals for staying ahead of their competitors.

Nature of Intrapreneurship

1. **Innovation-Driven**: Intrapreneurs focus on creating new products, services, or processes that enhance the company's competitive edge. They are often tasked with exploring and developing new ideas that can lead to significant improvements or entirely new business opportunities.
2. **Resource Utilization**: Unlike independent entrepreneurs, intrapreneurs work with the existing resources, infrastructure, and support systems of their organization. They use these resources to experiment, develop, and scale innovative solutions while navigating the corporate environment.

3. **Risk Management**: Intrapreneurs take on entrepreneurial risks, but these risks are generally mitigated by the organization's backing. They balance the potential rewards of their innovative efforts with the risks involved, often having access to company funding and support structures.
4. **Autonomy and Accountability**: Intrapreneurs typically operate with a degree of autonomy, allowing them to pursue new ideas and approaches. However, they are also accountable for their results, with their performance often measured against predefined goals and metrics.
5. **Cultural Impact**: Intrapreneurship can significantly impact organizational culture by fostering a climate of innovation and continuous improvement. It encourages employees to think creatively, challenge the status quo, and contribute to the company's strategic goals.
6. **Cross-Functional Collaboration**: Intrapreneurs often work across different departments, collaborating with various teams to bring their ideas to fruition. This cross-functional approach helps integrate innovative solutions into the organization's broader operations and strategies.
7. **Leadership and Vision**: Intrapreneurs possess leadership qualities and a visionary mindset, enabling them to champion new initiatives and drive them forward. They often act as change agents within their organizations, inspiring others and leading by example.

Role of Entrepreneurs/ entrepreneurships in the Economic Development

1. **Employment opportunities:** Entrepreneurs employ labour for managing their business activities and provides employment opportunities to a large number of people. They remove unemployment problem.

2. **Balanced Regional Development:** Government promotes decentralized development of industries as most of the incentives are granted for establishing industries in backward and rural areas. Thus, the entrepreneurs to avail the benefits establish industries in backward and rural areas They remove regional disparities and bring balanced regional development. They also help to reduce the problems of congestion, slums,

sanitation and pollution in cities by providing employment and income to people living in rural areas. They help in improving the standard of living of the people residing in suburban and rural areas.

3. Mobilization of Local Resources: Entrepreneurs help to mobilize and utilize local resources like small savings and talents of relatives and friends, which might otherwise remain idle and unutilized. Thus they help in effective utilization of resources.

4. Optimization of Capital: Entrepreneurs aim to get quick return on investment. They act as a stabilizing force by providing high output capital ratio as well as high employment capital ratio.

5. Promotion of Exports: Entrepreneurs reduce the pressure on the country's balance of payments by exporting their goods they earn valuable foreign exchange through exports.

6. Consumer Demands: Entrepreneurs produce a wide range of products required by consumers. They meet the demand of the consumers without creating a shortage for goods.

7. Social Advantage: Entrepreneurs help in the development of the society by providing employment to people and paves for independent living. They encourage democracy and self-governance. They are adept in distributing national income in more efficient and equitable manner among the various participants of the society.

8. Increase Per Capita Income: Entrepreneurs help to increase the per capita income of the country in various ways and facilitate development of backward areas and weaker sections of the society.

9. Capital formation: A country can attain economic development only when there is more amount of investment and production. Entrepreneurs help in channelizing their savings and savings of the public to productive resources by establishing enterprises. They promote capital formation by channelizing the savings of public to productive resources.

10. Growth of capital market: Entrepreneurs raises money for running their business through shares and debentures. Trading of shares and debentures by the public with the help of financial services sector leads to capital market growth.

11. Growth of infrastructure: The infrastructure development of any country determines the economic development of a country, Entrepreneurs by establishing their enterprises in rural and backward areas influence the government to develop the infrastructure of those areas.

12. Development of Trader: Entrepreneurs play an important role in the promotion of domestic trade and foreign trade. They avail assistance from various financial institutions in the form of cash credit, trade credit, overdraft, short term loans, secured loans and unsecured loans and lead to the development of the trade in the country.

13. Economic Integration: Entrepreneur reduces the concentration of power in a few hands by creating employment opportunities and through equitable distribution of income. Entrepreneurs promote economic integration in the country by adopting certain economic policies and laws framed by the government. They help in removing the disparity between the rich and the poor by adopting the rules and regulation framed by the government for the effective functioning of business in the country.

14. Inflow of Foreign Capital: Entrepreneurs help to attract funds from individuals and institutions residing in foreign countries for their businesses.

Importance of Entrepreneurship Development

The entrepreneurship development is needed on the following grounds

1. Optimum Utilisation of Resources Natural resources are getting depleted over a period of time. Some of the resources are almost scarce and it is the responsibility of the entrepreneurs to identify the alternative sources of supply of resources and also to make use of the existing resources without doing much harm to the environment

2. Improved Standard of Living The living conditions of the people could be improved through planned entrepreneurship development programme. Entrepreneurs use the latest technology and manufacture those products which are essential to all people at the lowest cost and thereby try to improve the living standar4 of the people.

3. Ensure Industrialisation A country is said to be advanced if there is an existence of adequate industrial units of big and small in size. The existing entrepreneurship development programmes create a congenial atmosphere for the aspiring and young entrepreneurs to come forward to set up industrial units especially in the industrially backward regions.

4. Innovation is the gateway Innovation takes place in all fields activities. The application of computers enable businessmen and Government to expedite their business activities. Marked improvement has been taken place in the filed of communication due to the application of innovative technology.

5. Allow Global Market Entry Entrepreneurship' development enables the manufactures to manufacture products of international quality and thereby try to enter into the global market and compete with the products of other nations.

Entrepreneurship Process

The entrepreneurial process is the sequence of steps and activities involved in starting and managing a new venture. It encompasses the identification of opportunities, gathering resources, creating a business plan, launching the venture, and managing its growth and development

1. Idea Generation and Opportunity Recognition

- **Creativity and Innovation:** The process begins with creativity, where entrepreneurs brainstorm potential ideas. These ideas often stem from personal experiences, market gaps, or emerging trends. Innovation plays a crucial role here as entrepreneurs think of novel solutions or improvements over existing products and services.
- **Opportunity Recognition:** Not all ideas are viable opportunities. Entrepreneurs assess whether the idea has the potential to create value. This involves understanding market needs, customer pain points, and the competitive landscape.
- **Initial Research:** Early research helps in identifying the market size, potential customer base, and existing competitors. Entrepreneurs might conduct informal surveys or gather feedback from potential customers to validate the idea.

2. Feasibility Analysis and Planning

Before launching a new venture, entrepreneurs need to evaluate the potential and viability of their ideas. This process is called feasibility analysis, and it involves assessing various aspects of the proposed business, such as the market, the industry, the product or service, the financials, and the operations. Feasibility analysis helps entrepreneurs to:

- Identify the strengths and weaknesses of their ideas and make necessary adjustments or improvements.
- Determine the level of demand and competition for their product or service and devise effective marketing strategies.
- Estimate the costs and revenues of their business and evaluate the profitability and sustainability of their venture.
- Identify the resources and capabilities required to operate their business and plan the operational processes and activities.
- Reduce the risks and uncertainties associated with their venture and increase the chances of success.

- **Market Research:** A thorough market analysis is conducted to understand the target market, segmentation, customer behavior, and industry trends. This helps in validating the demand for the product or service.
- **Technical Feasibility:** Entrepreneurs assess whether the idea can be technically executed with the available resources and technology. This includes analyzing the production process, supply chain, and required expertise.
- **Financial Feasibility:** This involves creating financial projections, estimating costs, revenue, and profitability. Entrepreneurs assess the initial capital requirements, break-even point, and potential return on investment (ROI).
- **Risk Assessment:** Identifying potential risks and challenges is crucial. Entrepreneurs evaluate economic, market, operational, and financial risks, and develop strategies to mitigate them.

3. Business Plan Development

A business plan refers to a formal statement of plans of an enterprise. It explains business goals of the enterprise and means to achieve those goals.

It seeks to address the strengths, weaknesses, opportunities, and threats of starting a venture. It involves

- **Executive Summary:** A concise overview of the business idea, objectives, and key strategies. This section is often critical in attracting investors and partners.
- **Business Model:** Entrepreneurs outline how the business will make money, detailing the value proposition, revenue streams, customer segments, and cost structure.
- **Marketing Plan:** A detailed strategy on how to reach and engage the target audience. This includes market positioning, pricing strategy, distribution channels, promotional tactics, and sales strategy.
- **Operational Plan:** A roadmap of how the business will operate day-to-day, including production, supply chain management, quality control, and customer service.
- **Financial Plan:** Detailed financial statements, including income statements, balance sheets, cash flow projections, and a break-even analysis. This section often includes funding requirements and proposed use of funds.
- **Legal and Organizational Structure:** The legal structure of the business (e.g., LLC, corporation), and an organizational chart detailing roles and responsibilities within the company.

4. Funding and Resource Mobilization

Successful entrepreneurial processes require entrepreneurs and teams to mobilize a wide array of resources quickly and efficiently. This requires an understanding of cash flow needs, break-even time frames, and other details. Different sources of funds are

- **Bootstrapping:** Entrepreneurs often start by using personal savings or reinvesting profits into the business. Bootstrapping helps maintain control but might limit growth.
- **External Funding:** If additional capital is needed, entrepreneurs may seek funding from external sources such as:

- ◦ **Angel Investors:** Individuals who provide capital for startups, often in exchange for equity.
- ◦ **Venture Capitalists:** Firms that invest in high-potential startups in exchange for equity, often providing mentorship and connections.
- ◦ **Bank Loans:** Traditional loans from financial institutions, which require repayment with interest.
- ◦ **Crowdfunding:** Raising small amounts of money from a large number of people, usually through online platforms.

- **Resource Mobilization:** Securing non-financial resources such as office space, technology, equipment, and human resources. This also includes building a strong team with the necessary skills and experience.

5. Business Launch

This is the process of getting the business to market. The stages involved are

- **Product Development:** Creating the product or service, often starting with a Minimum Viable Product (MVP) to test the market with the most essential features. Iterative development allows for refinement based on customer feedback.
- **Market Entry:** Launching the product or service to the market. This involves implementing the marketing plan, reaching out to early adopters, and creating initial sales. Entrepreneurs often use promotional strategies like soft launches, introductory offers, and targeted advertising.
- **Customer Acquisition:** Building a customer base is critical at this stage. Entrepreneurs focus on lead generation, customer relationship management, and building brand loyalty.
- **Feedback and Iteration:** Collecting customer feedback is essential to refine the product, improve user experience, and address any issues. Continuous improvement helps in maintaining product relevance and customer satisfaction.

6. Growth and Scaling

This is the procedure of growing and extending the business.

- **Market Penetration:** Increasing market share in the existing market by attracting more customers and increasing sales. This might involve more aggressive marketing, competitive pricing, or enhancing product features.
- **Market Expansion:** Entering new geographical markets or targeting new customer segments. This could involve adapting the product or service to meet the needs of different demographics or regions.
- **Product Line Expansion:** Introducing new products or services that complement the existing offerings, catering to a broader range of customer needs.
- **Operational Scaling:** Expanding operational capacity to meet growing demand. This could involve automating processes, increasing production capacity, hiring more staff, or expanding supply chains.
- **Investment in Technology:** Leveraging technology to optimize operations, improve customer experience, and enhance decision-making processes.

7. Maturity and Stabilization

- **Business Optimization:** Fine-tuning operations to maximize efficiency and profitability. This involves continuous process improvement, cost management, and quality assurance.
- **Brand Building:** Strengthening brand equity through consistent customer experience, reputation management, and strategic marketing efforts.
- **Diversification:** Exploring new business opportunities, either by diversifying product offerings or entering new industries. This reduces dependency on a single revenue stream and mitigates risk.
- **Sustainability:** Entrepreneurs focus on long-term sustainability by adopting practices that ensure the business can thrive in the long term, including environmental, social, and governance (ESG) considerations.

8. *Exit Strategy*

- **Merger or Acquisition:** Selling the business to another company or merging with another entity. This allows the entrepreneur to realize the value created and potentially stay involved in a leadership role.
- **Initial Public Offering (IPO):** Taking the company public by offering shares on the stock market. This can provide significant capital and increase the company's visibility and credibility.
- **Succession Planning:** Preparing the business for transfer to the next generation of leaders, whether within the family or to professional managers.
- **Liquidation:** In cases where the business is not viable, liquidation may be necessary. This involves selling off assets to pay debts and winding down operations.
- **Reflection and Learning:** Entrepreneurs often reflect on their journey, extracting lessons and insights that can be applied to future ventures. Many go on to mentor other entrepreneurs or start new businesses.

Business Model

A business model is a high-level plan for how a business will earn and maximize **profits**. Business models establish whether a company will offer a product or service, be online or brick and mortar, or sell to businesses vs directly to consumers, or a hybrid between several traditional business models. A business model defines how a company creates, delivers, and captures value. It acts as a blueprint for the operations, strategies, and potential profitability of a business. Business models are important for both new and established businesses. They help companies attract investment, recruit talent, and motivate management and staff. It is more than just an operational plan; it represents how a company does business. Understanding and effectively developing a business model is essential for any business looking to thrive in today's competitive marketplace.

Key Components of a Business Model

1. Value Proposition

The value proposition is at the heart of a business model, defining the unique benefits and advantages that a company offers to its customers. It answers the question of why a customer would choose one product or service over another.

This aspect is not just about the product or service itself but also includes elements like customer service, brand reputation, and overall customer experience. For example, Apple's value proposition is not just in its innovative products but also in its ecosystem and brand prestige.

2. Revenue Streams

When most people think of a business model, they tend to think of its revenue streams. Revenue streams represent the various ways a business makes money. These can include direct sales, subscription fees, licensing, and advertising. A diversified revenue stream can help buffer a business against market fluctuations. It can also help them reach their financial goals because some revenue streams can be maxed out fairly quickly.

For example, a software company might earn revenue through direct software sales. However, they may choose to add a subscription service to capture the customers not willing to pay full price to own the software. They may also decide to offer customization services because an enterprise may need that while a consumer may not.

3. Market Segmentation

Market segmentation involves dividing a target market into manageable groups. Businesses can segment their market by demographics, geography, behavior, or other criteria. Understanding these segments allows companies to tailor their offerings and marketing strategies to meet the specific needs of each group. For example, a cosmetic company might segment its market into different age groups, offering different products to teenagers, adults, and seniors.

4. Cost Structure

This component outlines all costs involved in operating a business model. It includes fixed costs like rent and salaries, and variable costs such as materials and logistics. Understanding the cost structure is crucial for pricing strategies and financial planning. Businesses must strive for a cost structure that allows them to be competitive yet profitable.

5. Business Processes

Business processes are the collection of activities that produce a product or deliver a service. These can include manufacturing processes, marketing activities, and customer service operations. Efficient and effective business processes are key to delivering on the value proposition and maintaining a competitive advantage. For example, Amazon's efficient logistics and distribution processes are central to its ability to offer quick delivery services.

6. Resources

Resources are the assets a company needs to create and offer its value proposition, reach its market, and deliver on its business processes. These can be physical (like buildings and machinery), intellectual (like patents and trademarks), human (skills and expertise), or financial. Effective management of these resources is crucial for the success of a business model. For example, a technology startup might rely heavily on human resources in the form of software developers and engineers.

7. Customer Relationships

This aspect defines how a company interacts with its customers throughout the customer journey. It involves not just acquiring and retaining customers but also enhancing customer experiences and engagement. Companies need to establish and maintain positive relationships with their customers, as this can lead to increased customer loyalty and word-of-mouth referrals. For example, a brand like Nike fosters customer relationships through community-building efforts and personalized marketing.

8. Distribution Channels

Distribution channels are the pathways through which a company delivers its products or services to customers. This can include physical channels like retail stores, or digital channels like e-commerce websites or mobile apps. The choice of distribution channels can significantly impact a business's reach and efficiency. For instance, digital-first brands may rely primarily on e-commerce platforms to reach a global audience.

9. Key Partnerships

Many business models rely on partnerships with other companies to operate effectively. These partnerships can include suppliers, distributors, or even complementary businesses. Collaborations can help businesses expand their capabilities, reach new markets, and share risks. For example, a car manufacturer might partner with technology firms to develop new in-car entertainment systems.

Importance of Entrepreneurship Ecosystem

The entrepreneurial ecosystem is defined as a community that is made of multiple factors independent from each other, which interact with themselves in a geographical area and evolve. The purpose is to promote the creation of new businesses. The entrepreneurship ecosystem is the network of interconnected factors, organizations, and processes that support and nurture entrepreneurial activity within a specific region or industry. It includes elements such as access to finance, mentorship, education, infrastructure, regulatory frameworks, and cultural attitudes towards entrepreneurship. The importance of a strong entrepreneurship ecosystem cannot be overstated, as it plays a crucial role in fostering innovation, economic growth, and social development.

1.Fosters Innovation and Creativity

- **Encouragement of New Ideas:** A vibrant entrepreneurship ecosystem encourages the generation of new ideas by providing an environment where creativity is valued and supported. It connects entrepreneurs with resources such as R&D institutions, incubators, and accelerators that can help transform ideas into viable products or services.
- **Risk-Taking Culture:** In a supportive ecosystem, the culture encourages calculated risk-taking, where entrepreneurs are not deterred by the fear of failure. This leads to more experimentation and innovation.

2. Economic Growth and Job Creation

- **Business Formation:** A healthy ecosystem facilitates the creation of new businesses, which in turn contribute to economic growth. Startups and small businesses are often the engines of job creation, driving employment and reducing unemployment rates.
- **Increased Productivity:** Innovative businesses enhance productivity across industries by introducing new technologies, processes, and business models. This leads to more efficient resource use and higher

economic output.

3. *Access to Capital*

- **Funding Opportunities:** A strong ecosystem provides entrepreneurs with access to various forms of capital, such as venture capital, angel investors, government grants, and crowdfunding. This financial support is essential for startups to scale and succeed.
- **Diverse Funding Sources:** In a mature ecosystem, entrepreneurs can tap into a diverse array of funding sources, reducing dependency on traditional financing methods and increasing the chances of securing the necessary resources.

4. *Supportive Infrastructure*

- **Physical Infrastructure:** A well-developed infrastructure, including co-working spaces, research labs, and technology parks, provides entrepreneurs with the facilities they need to develop and test their ideas.
- **Digital Infrastructure:** Access to high-speed internet, digital platforms, and e-commerce facilities allows entrepreneurs to reach wider markets and streamline their operations.
- **Logistical Support:** Efficient transportation and logistics networks enable entrepreneurs to manage supply chains effectively and deliver products to customers in a timely manner.

5. *Access to Talent and Skills Development*

- **Educational Institutions:** Universities and technical schools within the ecosystem provide the necessary education and training, equipping aspiring entrepreneurs with the skills they need to succeed.

- **Mentorship and Networks:** Access to experienced mentors, advisors, and industry experts is crucial for guiding entrepreneurs through the challenges of starting and growing a business. Networking events, incubators, and accelerators facilitate these connections.
- **Skilled Workforce:** A strong ecosystem attracts and retains talent, providing startups with access to a skilled and motivated workforce that can drive innovation and growth.

6. *Supportive Legal and Regulatory Framework*

- **Ease of Doing Business:** An ecosystem with clear, supportive, and efficient regulatory processes lowers the barriers to entry for new businesses. This includes simplifying business registration, providing legal protections for intellectual property, and ensuring fair competition.
- **Policy Support:** Government policies that support entrepreneurship, such as tax incentives, startup-friendly regulations, and grants, create an environment where entrepreneurs can thrive.
- **Intellectual Property Rights:** Protecting intellectual property (IP) rights is crucial for encouraging innovation. A strong IP framework gives entrepreneurs the confidence that their ideas and innovations will be safeguarded.

7. *Market Access and Globalization*

- **Local and Global Markets:** A strong ecosystem provides entrepreneurs with access to both local and global markets. Trade agreements, export incentives, and international networking opportunities help businesses expand beyond their domestic markets.
- **Market Information:** Entrepreneurs benefit from access to market research, industry trends, and customer insights, which helps them tailor their products and strategies to meet market demands.

8. Cultural Support and Societal Attitudes

- **Entrepreneurial Culture:** A culture that celebrates entrepreneurship encourages more people to pursue entrepreneurial careers. Societal attitudes that view entrepreneurs as innovators and risk-takers contribute to a positive environment for new ventures.
- **Community Support:** A supportive community, including peer networks and local champions, can provide moral support, shared experiences, and collaborative opportunities, which are vital for the mental and emotional well-being of entrepreneurs.

9. Reduces Failure Rate

- **Guidance and Resources:** A strong ecosystem provides entrepreneurs with access to guidance, resources, and support systems that can help them navigate challenges and avoid common pitfalls. This reduces the likelihood of failure and increases the chances of long-term success.
- **Learning from Failure:** Even when businesses do fail, a supportive ecosystem encourages learning from failures. Entrepreneurs are often able to start new ventures with the lessons learned, contributing to a cycle of continuous improvement and innovation.

10. Sustainability and Social Impact

- **Support for Social Enterprises:** Ecosystems that support entrepreneurship also foster the growth of social enterprises that address societal challenges such as poverty, inequality, and environmental degradation.
- **Sustainable Practices:** Entrepreneurs in a strong ecosystem are more likely to adopt sustainable business practices, driven by access to knowledge, resources, and a market that values sustainability.

11. Resilience in Economic Downturns

- **Cushioning Against Crises:** A diverse and dynamic entrepreneurship ecosystem can act as a buffer during economic downturns. By fostering innovation and adaptability, the ecosystem helps businesses pivot and survive in challenging times.
- **Rapid Recovery:** After economic shocks, regions with strong entrepreneurship ecosystems often recover more quickly due to the adaptability and innovation driven by their entrepreneurial ventures.

CHAPTER FOUR

BUSINESS DEVELOPMENT THROUGH ENTREPRENEURSHIP

Setting up of a business unit

The potential entrepreneur would become an entrepreneur only when he owns an enterprise. The business enterprise to be set up can be a manufacturing venture, a trading firm or a service establishment. The manufacturing venture includes the steps required for setting up a trading firm or a service establishment also. The steps in setting up a small unit are as follows:

Steps Involved

1. **Decision to be Self-employed**: This is the most crucial decision a person has to take shunning wage employment and opting for self-employment or entrepreneurship. He should know the advantages and risks of entrepreneurship.

2. **Analysing strengths, weaknesses:** The potential entrepreneur has to analyse his strength, weaknesses, while deciding to go for entrepreneur career. This analysis enables him to know what type and size of business would be the most suitable. The strengths and weaknesses will vary from person to person.

3. **Availability of own money:** No business can be created, with zero capital. The 'Own Money' concept means the funds available with an

entrepreneur from his own source or family or friends. The size of the unit depends on the availability of 'Own Money' in short-term and long-term.

4. Scanning of business environment: It is always essential on the part of an entrepreneur to study and understand the prevailing business environment in which they operate particularly the industrial policy, economic policy, licensing policy, legal environment, technological environment and above all the markets. In order to ensure success of his enterprise, the entrepreneur should scan the business opportunities and threats in the environment. He should study the administrative frame work, procedures, policies, rules and regulations and other formalities implemented by the government.

5. Training: The person should undergo training for developing skills for entrepreneurship and developing technical, conceptual and managerial skills. Before going to start the enterprise, the potential entrepreneur must assess his own deficiencies, which he can compensate through training. He can attend the Entrepreneurial Development Programmes (EDP) conducted by institutes like DIC, SISI, TCOs, SBI, etc., These institutes are providing tailor-made Entrepreneurship Development Programmes (EDP) and skill upgradation training programmes for the benefit of the new entrepreneur, existing entrepreneurs and for the employees of the small-scale industries.

6. Product Selection: The next step and the most important step is to decide what business to venture into, the product or range of products that shall be selected for manufacture and in what quantity. The level of activity will help in determining the size of business and thus form of ownership. One could generate as many project ideas as one can through environment scanning and short list a few of them. Closely examine with the help of opportunity analysis each one of them and zero in on to the final product or products.

7. Market Survey: It is always convenient to manufacture an item but difficult to sell. So it is prudent or rational on the part of the entrepreneur to survey the market thoroughly before embarking upon production and ensure that the product chosen is in sufficient demand and is preferably in the growth phase of a product life cycle. Market survey means systematic collection of data by the entrepreneur about the product for manufacture, demand-supply lag, extent of competition, frequency of demand, pattern and design of demand, its potential share in the market, pricing, distribution policy etc. The principle is to produce what actually people demand. The entrepreneur can contact for this the concerned authorities.

8. Selection of form of ownership/organisation: A firm can be constituted as proprietorship, partnership, limited company (public or private) or co-operative society. This will depend upon the type, purpose and size of entrepreneur's business. One may also decide on the form of ownership, on the basis of resources in hand or from the point of view of investment.

9. Location: The next step will be to decide the location where the unit is to be established. Will it be hired or owned? The size of plot, covered and open area and the exact site will have to be decided. Decision about the location of unit is very important. Location determines the success or failure of the enterprise. Location is selected after considering such factors such as nearness to market, sources of material and labour, modern infrastructural facilities etc.

10. Technology: To manufacture any item, technology is used. Information on all available technologies should be collected by the entrepreneur and the most suitable one should be identified. This will also be useful to determine the type of machinery and equipment to be installed. Many institutions of government like DIC, TCO etc. research laboratories, R & D. divisions of big industries and certain consultancy agencies provide the manufacturing know-how.

11. Machinery and equipment: Having chosen the technology, the machinery and equipment required for manufacturing, the chosen products have to be decided, suppliers have to be identified and their costs have to be estimated. One may have to plan well in advance for machinery and equipment especially if it has to be procured from outside the town, state or country.

12. Preparation of Project Report (Business Plan): After deciding the form of ownership, location, technology for manufacturing, machinery and equipment, the entrepreneur should be ready to prepare his project report or the feasibility study. The economic viability and the technical feasibility of the product selected have to be established through a project report. A project report that may now be prepared will be helpful in formulating the production, marketing, financial and management plans. It will also be useful in obtaining finance, shed, power connection, water connection, raw material quotas, etc. The entrepreneur has to consider the guidelines given by the Planning Commission in preparing the project report. The project report should indicate the vision of the promoter and short term and long term aspects of the project implementation.

13. Project appraisal: Project appraisal means the assessment of a project. It is a technique for ex-ante analysis of a scheme or project while preparing to set up an enterprise, the entrepreneur has to carefully appraise the project from the stand point of economic, financial, technical, market, social and managerial aspects to arrive at the most socially-feasible enterprise. To avail the finance from the banks and financial institutions, a comprehensive appraisal of projects carrying technoeconomic feasibility aspects should be undertaken by the entrepreneur. Thus a project which is selected should be technically feasible and economically viable and then only it will be bankable.

For this the following appraisals can be performed at the preliminary level;

(a) Economic appraisal
(b) Financial appraisal
(c) Technical appraisal
(d) Management appraisal
(e) Organisational appraisal
(f) Operational appraisal
(g) Market appraisal

14. Finance: Finance is the life-blood of the enterprise. Entrepreneur has to take certain steps and follow specified norms of the financial institutions and banks to obtain money or finance. A number of financial agencies provide capital assistance and venture capital for starting an enterprise. There are some agencies which provide financial assistance on concessional rates. Under PMRY and REGP schemes, financial assistance and subsidies are being provided to the persons who want to set up their own enterprise, which obviates the need for margin money.

15. Provisional Registration: It is always worthwhile to get the unit registered with the government. The entrepreneur has to obtain the prescribed application form for provisional registration from DIC or Directorate of Industries. After having duly filled in the application form, he has to submit the application with all relevant documents in the local DIC or Directorate of Industries. This will enable the entrepreneur to avail various government facilities, assistance and incentives schemes including financial assistance from NSIC, SFCs and KVIC.

16. Technical know-how: In some cases, technical know-how may be arranged for setting up enterprises. This can be arranged through TC0s, NSIC, SSIDC, DIC, private consultants, SISI, ED-institutes, foreign collaborators, India Investment Centre and Industry etc. Facilities are also available to SSI for making variety of technical know-how arrangements including turn-key jobs.

17. Power and Water Connection: The sites where the enterprise will be located, should either have adequate power connections or this should be arranged. The entrepreneur can calculate the total power requirement and determine the nearest pole from which power will be given to the enterprise, as it can materially affect the installation cost. There are two categories of power, namely, the Low Tension (LT) and High Tension (HT). A consumer can avail LT only if the connected load is 75 HP and below. If the connected load is between 75 HP and 130 HP, the consumer has the option to avail either LT supply or HT supply. Most of the SSI units fall under the LT category. HT power supply may mean additional investment in transformer and sub-station. Most states, need a No Objection Certificate from the concerned Pollution Control Authorities, before the power connection. Similarly, the water connection will have to be obtained or provision should be made for adequate water supply to the firm.

18. Installation of machinery: Having completed the above formalities, the next step is to procure machinery and begin its installation as per the plant layout.

19. Insurance: It is necessary to have adequate insurance for the fixed assets at this stage and later on for the current assets as well.

20. Recruitment of manpower: Once machines are installed, the need for manpower arises to run them. So, the quantum and type of manpower (skilled, semi-skilled, unskilled, administrative etc.) is to be decided. The sources of getting desired labour are also important. This follows the recruitment, training and placement.

21. Procurement of raw materials: Raw materials are the important ingredients for running an enterprise. The labour will require raw materials to work upon the installed machinery. These materials may be procured indigenously or may have to be imported by the entrepreneur. The entrepreneur has to identify the cheap and assured sources of supply of raw materials for running his own enterprise. Government agencies can assist in case the raw materials are scarce or imported.

22. Production: The unit established should have an organisational set-up. To operate optimally, the organisation should employ its manpower, machinery and methods effectively. There should not be any wastage of manpower, machinery and materials. If items are exported, then the product and its packaging must be attractive. Production of the proposed item should be taken up in two stages

i. **Trial production: Trial production will help tackling problems confronted in production and test marketing of the product. This will reduce the chances of losses in the eventuality of mistakes in project conception.**
ii. **Commercial Production: Commercial production should be commenced only after the successfully launching the product at the test marketing stage.**

23. Marketing: Marketing is the most important activity as far as the entrepreneurial development is concerned. Various aspects like how to reach the customer, distribution channels, commission structure, pricing, advertising, publicity etc. have to be decided by the entrepreneur. Like production, marketing should also be attempted cautiously, that is, in two stages namely: (i) Test stage (ii) Commercial marketing stage. Test marketing is necessary to save the enterprise from going into disrepute in case the product launched is not well accepted by the customers. It will also assist the entrepreneur in carrying out modifications or additions in designs and features of the product. Having successfully test marketed the product, commercial marketing can be undertaken. The entrepreneur can contact the Small Industries Marketing Corporation.

24. Quality Assurance: Before marketing, the product quality certification from BIS (Bureau of Indian Standard) / AGMARK / HALLMARK etc. should be obtained depending upon the product. If there is no quality standards specified for the products, the entrepreneur should evolve his own quality control parameters. After all, quality ensures long-term success.

25. Permanent Registration: After the small scale unit goes into production and marketing, it becomes eligible to get permanent registration based on its provisional registration from DIC or Directorate of Industries.

26. Market Research: Once the product or service is introduced in the market, there is strong need for continuous market research to assess needs and areas for modification, upgradation and growth. Market becomes the waterloo for most SSI entrepreneurs as they ignore this vital function. Initial success should not lure the entrepreneur into a sense of complacency.

27. Monitoring: Periodical monitoring and evaluation not only of markets but also production, quality and profitability helps in knowing where the firm stands in comparison to performance envisaged in the business plan. It also identifies direction of future growth.

Entrepreneurship Challenges

1.

Access to Capital

Securing adequate funding is often one of the biggest challenges for entrepreneurs, particularly in the early stages of a venture. Explore diverse funding options, build a strong business case, and network with potential investors. Consider bootstrapping or crowdfunding as alternative funding methods.

2. Market Competition

Entering a competitive market can be daunting, especially when established players dominate. New ventures may struggle to differentiate themselves and capture market share.

Solution: Focus on a unique value proposition, identify niche markets, and leverage innovative marketing strategies to stand out from competitors.

3. Managing Cash Flow

Maintaining positive cash flow is critical for the survival of a new venture. Cash flow problems can arise from delayed payments, high operational costs, or unexpected expenses.

Solution: Implement effective cash flow management practices, such as budgeting, forecasting, and closely monitoring receivables and payables. Consider securing a line of credit for emergencies.

4. Hiring and Retaining Talent

Attracting and retaining skilled employees can be difficult for startups, which may not offer the same level of job security, benefits, or salaries as established companies.

Solution: Build a strong company culture, offer equity or profit-sharing options, and provide opportunities for growth and development to attract top talent.

5. Time Management

Entrepreneurs often wear many hats and have to juggle multiple responsibilities, leading to time management challenges.

Solution: Prioritize tasks, delegate responsibilities, and use productivity tools to manage time effectively. Focus on high-impact activities that drive business growth.

6. Building a Customer Base

Gaining the trust and loyalty of customers is crucial but can be challenging, especially for new and unknown brands.

Solution: Deliver exceptional customer service, build strong relationships with early adopters, and use word-of-mouth marketing and social proof to build credibility.

7. Regulatory Compliance

Navigating complex regulatory requirements can be a significant hurdle, particularly in heavily regulated industries.

Solution: Stay informed about industry regulations, seek legal advice, and ensure compliance with all relevant laws and standards from the outset.

8. Maintaining Work-Life Balance

The demands of starting and running a new venture can lead to burnout if entrepreneurs do not maintain a healthy work-life balance.

Solution: Set boundaries, schedule time for personal activities, and delegate tasks to avoid becoming overwhelmed. Prioritize self-care to sustain long-term productivity.

9. Adapting to Market Changes

Markets are dynamic, and sudden changes in consumer behavior, economic conditions, or technology can pose challenges for new ventures.

Solution: Stay agile, continuously monitor market trends, and be ready to pivot the business model or strategy in response to changes.

10. Dealing with Uncertainty and Risk

Entrepreneurship involves inherent risks and uncertainties, including the possibility of failure, financial loss, and unexpected challenges.

Solution: Develop a risk management plan, conduct regular SWOT (Strengths, Weaknesses, Opportunities, Threats) analysis, and build a resilient mindset to navigate uncertainty.

Project Ideas

It is the first and foremost task of an entrepreneur to find out suitable business which is feasible and promising and which merit further examination and appraisal. Therefore, he has to first search for a sound workable business idea and give a practical shape to his idea. While doing so, the entrepreneur has to tackle the various problems from time to time to achieve the ultimate success. Since the good project ideas are elusive, a variety of sources should be tapped to stimulate the generation of project ideas.

Sources of Project Ideas

Project ideas could originate from the various sources viz., Success story of a friend/relatives Experience of others in manufacture/sale of product Examining the inputs and outputs of industries Plan outlays and government guidelines Suggestions of financial institutions and developmental agencies Investigation of local materials and resources Economic and social trend of the economy New technological developments Project profiles and industrial potential surveys Visits to trade fairs Unfulfilled psychological needs Possibility of reviving sick units

The various sources from which the project idea can be generated are explained below:

1. Analyse the Performance of Existing Industries

A study of existing industries in terms of their profitability and capacity utilisation is helpful. The analysis of profitability and break-even level of various industries indicates promising investment opportunities. Opportunities which are profitable and relatively risk free. An examination of capacity utilisation of various industries provides information about the potential for further investment. Such a study becomes more useful if it is done region wise, particularly for products which have high transportation costs.

2. Examine the Inputs and Outputs of Industries

An analysis of the inputs required for various industries may throw up project ideas. Opportunities exist when i) materials purchased parts, or supplies are presently being procured from different sources with attendant time lag and transportation costs and ii) several firms produce internally some components/parts which can be supplied at a lower cost by a single manufactures who can enjoy economies of scale. A study of the output structure of existing industries may reveal opportunities for further processing of output or even processing of waste.

3. Examine Imports and Exports

An analysis of import statistics for a period of five to seven years is helpful in understanding the trend of imports of various goods and the potential for import substitution. Indigenous manufacture of goods currently imported is advantageous for several reasons:

· it improves the balance of payments situation

· it provides market for supporting industries and services

· it generates employment Likewise, an examination of export statistics is useful in learning about the export possibilities of various products.

4. Plan Outlays and Government Guidelines

The government plays a very important role in our economy. Its proposed outlays in different sector provides useful pointers toward investment opportunities. They indicate the potential demand for goods and service required by different sectors.

5. Suggestions of Financial Institutions and Developmental Agencies

In a bid to promote development of industries in their respective states, state financial corporations state industrial development corporations and other developmental bodies conduct studies, prepare feasibility reports and offer suggestions to potential entrepreneur. The suggestions of these bodies are helpful in identifying promising projects.

6. Investigate Local Materials and Resources

A search for project ideas may begin with an investigation into local resources and skills, various ways of adding value to locally available materials may be examined. Similarly, the skills of local artisans may suggest products that may be profitably produced and marketed.

7. Analyse Economic and Social Trends

A study of economic and social trends is helpful in projecting demand for various goods and services. Changing economic conditions provide new business opportunities. A great awareness of the value of time is dawning on the public. Hence the demand for time saving products like prepared food items, ovens and powered vehicles has been increasing. Another change that we are witnessing is that the desire for leisure and recreational activities has been increasing. This has caused a growth in the market for recreational products and services.

8. Identify Unfulfilled Psychological Needs

For well established, multi brand product groups like bathing soaps, detergents, cosmetics and tooth pastes, the question to be asked is not whether there is an opportunity to manufacture something to satisfy an actual physical need but whether there are certain psychological needs of consumers which are presently unfulfilled. To find whether such an opportunity exists, the technique of spectrum analysis may be followed. This analysis is done somewhat as follows. Important factors influencing brand choice are identified respect of the factors identified in step gaps which exist in relation to consumer psychological needs are identified.

9. Visit to Trade Fairs

Attending the National and International trade fairs provides an excellent opportunity to know about new products and new development. The above said sources of project ideas may be generated by the Government agencies, credit institutions, non-governmental organisations and also by public. The Govt. have largest resources and have the necessary information to generate project ideas and it plays a predominant role in this sphere. The government has the required facilities and manpower to conduct detailed studies which may lead to making investment decisions. Banks and other financial institutions are actively involved in sharing the social responsibility of achieving the national objectives of economic development. The co-operatives and nongovernmental organisations as well as individual entrepreneurs are now actively participated in identification of projects.

Generating Project Ideas

After clearing some of the initial misconceptions about ideas, it's time to look at the process involved with generating ideas. Generating ideas is an innovative and creative process. Initially it seems difficult to think of many ideas and it will take some time, not only in the beginning stages of the entrepreneurial venture but also throughout the life of the business. The process of generating ideas we are going to discuss where ideas come from, ways to generate ideas and the role of structured approach, analysis and intuition.

Ways to Generate Ideas

The different structured approaches that might be adopted to generate ideas are:

1. **Environment Scanning :**One of the important techniques that can be used to generate ideas is environment scanning, the screening of large amounts of information to detect emerging trends. A humongous amount of information from popular news magazines, reviews, government and consumer publications, trade publications, commercials, etc. will have to be scanned. The challenge in this method is not having too little information to scan, its having too much. It seems like a lot of effort to work but if you are serious about being a successful entrepreneur in action, it is energy well spent.

2. **Creativity and Creative Problem Solving** :Creativity is the ability to combine ideas in a unique way or to make unusual associations between the ideas. It means cross thinking by seeing new angles, connections and approaches. The role of creativity and creative problem solving as a structured technique for generating ideas is that a number of specific creative approaches can be used. For instance - (i) attribute listing - in which entrepreneur develops a new idea by looking at the positive or negative attributes of a product or a service and so on. (ii) free association – whereby, an entrepreneur develops a new idea through a chain of word associations etc.,

3. Brainstorming :A group of persons sit together and generate a number of business ideas by innovating alternative ways of meeting the needs and solving problems. It is usually an unstructured discussion in which one idea leads to another. This is a very productive method for generating as many ideas as possible.

4. Focus Groups: These groups of individuals provide information about proposed products or services in a structured setting. In a typical focus group, a moderator focuses the group discussion or whatever issues are being examined. For instance, a focus group might look at a proposed product and answer specific answer asked by the moderators. A focus group can provide an excellent way to generate new ideas and to screen proposed ideas and concepts.

5. Market Research: This is a method of gathering information about products/services that already exist in the market. A systematic and in-depth study is undertaken to obtain useful data to determine demand supply position for a particular product or service that is already available in the market. Such research will help in getting new ideas for products and services.

Business Plan

A business plan is an executive document that acts as a blueprint or roadmap for a business. It is quite necessary for new ventures seeking capital, expansion activities, or projects requiring additional capital. It is also important to remind the management, employees, and partners of what they represent.

A business plan is a comprehensive document that outlines a company's goals, strategies, and financial projections. It provides a detailed description of the business, including its products or services, target market, competitive landscape, and marketing and sales strategies. The plan also includes a financial section that forecasts revenue, expenses, and cash flow, as well as a funding request if the business is seeking investment.

Components of a Project Report/ business plan

Following are the contents of a project report:

1.General Information

A project report must provide information about the details of the industry to which the project belongs to. It must give information about the past experience, present status, problems and future prospects of the industry. It must give information about the product to be manufactured and the reasons for selecting the product if the proposed business is a manufacturing unit. It must spell out the demand for the product in the local, national and the global market. It should clearly identify the alternatives of business and should clarify the reasons for starting the business.

2. Executive Summary

A project report must state the objectives of the business and the methods through which the business can attain success. The overall picture of the business with regard to capital, operations, methods of functioning and execution of the business must be stated in the project report. It must mention the assumptions and the risks generally involved in the business.

3.Organization Summary

The project report should indicate the organization structure and pattern proposed for the unit. It must state whether the ownership is based on sole proprietorship, partnership or Joint Stock Company. It must provide information about the bio data of the promoters including financial soundness. The name, address, age qualification and experience of the proprietors or promoters of the proposed business must be stated in the project report.

4. Project Description A brief description of the project must be stated and must give details about the following:

Location of the site,
Raw material requirements,
Target of production,
Area required for the work shed,
Power requirements,
Fuel requirements,
Water requirements,
Employment requirements of skilled and unskilled labour,
Technology selected for the project,
Production process,
Projected production volumes, unit prices,
Pollution treatment plants required.

If the business is service oriented, then it must state the type of services rendered to customers. It should state the method of providing service to customers in detail.

5. Marketing Plan The project report must clearly state the total expected demand for the product. It must state the price at which the product can be sold in the market. It must also mention the strategies to be employed to capture the market. If any, after sale service is provided that must also be stated in the project. It must describe the mode of distribution of the product from the production unit to the market. Project report must state the following:

Type of customers,
Target markets,
Nature of market,
Market segmentation,
Future prospects of the market
Sales objectives,
Marketing Cost of the project,
Market share of proposed venture,
Demand for the product in the local, national and the global market,

It must indicate potential users of products and distribution channels to be used for distributing the product.

6. Capital Structure and operating cost The project report must describe the total capital requirements of the project. It must state the source of finance, it must also indicate the extent of owner's funds and borrowed funds. Working capital requirements must be stated and the source of supply should also be indicated in the project. Estimate of total project cost, must be broken down into land, construction of buildings and civil works, plant and machinery, miscellaneous fixed assets, preliminary and preoperative expenses and working capital. Proposed financial structure of venture must indicate the expected sources and terms of equity and debt financing. This section must also spell out the operating cost.

7. Management Plan The project report should state the following. a. Business experience of the promoters of the business, b. Details about the management team, c. Duties and responsibilities of team members, d. Current personnel needs of the organization, e. Methods of managing the business, f. Plans for hiring and training personnel, g. Programmes and policies of the management.

8. Financial Aspects In order to judge the profitability of the business a projected profit and loss account and balance sheet must be presented in the project report. It must show the estimated sales revenue, cost of production, gross profit and net profit likely to be earned by the proposed unit. In addition to the above, a projected balance sheet, cash flow statement and funds flow statement must be prepared every year and at least for a period of 3 to 5 years. The income statement and cash flow projections should include a three-year summary, detail by month for the first year, and detail by quarter for the second and third years. Breakeven point and rate of return on investment must be stated in the project report. The accounting system and the inventory control system will be used is generally addressed in this section of the project report. The project report must state whether the business is financially and economically viable.

9. **Technical Aspects** Project report provides information about the technology and technical aspects of a project. It covers information on Technology selected for the project, Production process, capacity of machinery, pollution control plants etc.

10.Project Implementation Every proposed business unit must draw a time table for the project. It must indicate the time within the activities involved in establishing the enterprise can be completed. Implementation schemes show the timetable envisaged for project preparation and completion.

11.Social responsibility

The proposed units draws inputs from the society. Hence its contribution to the society in the form of employment, income, exports and infrastructure. The output of the business must be indicated in the project report.

Need/Objectives/Purpose of Project Report/ business plan

1. **Selecting Best Investment Proposal**: Project report is an efficient tool for analyzing the status of any investment proposal. It shows the expected profitability and risk associated with the project and this way helps in choosing the best option.

2. **Approval of Project:** It is essential for registration or approval purposes of the proposed project. Different authorities like District industries center, Directorate of industries, government departments, etc. require project reports for giving approval.

3. Tracking: The Project report assists in tracking the current activities of the project. It helps team members and other stakeholders to check the project progress from time to time and helps in finding out any deviations against the original plan.

4. Visibility: Another important advantage of having the project report is that it gives full insight into the project. It gives a clear description of activities to be undertaken and avoids any confusion or disorder.

5. Risk Identification: Identification of risk is a significant step for the completion of every project. The project report enables in spotting the risk early and taking all corrective actions timely.

6. Cost Management: Project report helps in managing the expenses through regular reporting of all activities. It sets the standard cost of every operation in advance and helps in finding out any deviation in these costs through tracking of the project.

7. **Financial Assistance:** It is an important tool for availing financial assistance from financial institutions or fund providers. The project report enables financial institutions in judging the profitability of the proposed project and then takes the decision accordingly for approving the funds.

8. Test Business Soundness: Project report helps in testing the profitability and soundness of the proposed project. It tells the total estimated costs, possible income and risk associated with any proposal

Entrepreneurial marketing

Entrepreneurial marketing is a unique approach to marketing that is particularly suited to startups and small businesses. It differs from traditional marketing in its emphasis on innovation, agility, and resourcefulness. Entrepreneurs often operate with limited budgets, so they need to be creative and strategic in how they reach their target audience and build their brand.

Key Characteristics of Entrepreneurial Marketing:

1. Customer-Centric Focus:

Deep Understanding of the Customer: Entrepreneurs prioritize understanding their customers' needs, preferences, and pain points. This understanding guides product development, messaging, and marketing strategies.

Direct Interaction: Engaging directly with customers, through feedback loops, social media, or face-to-face interactions, allows entrepreneurs to build strong relationships and loyalty.

2. Innovation and Creativity:

Unconventional Tactics: Entrepreneurial marketing often involves unconventional tactics like guerrilla marketing, which uses surprise or unconventional methods to generate buzz.

Leveraging Digital Tools: Social media, content marketing, and email campaigns are often used innovatively to reach and engage audiences cost-effectively.

Experimentation: Entrepreneurs are often willing to experiment with different marketing channels and tactics to find what works best, allowing for quick adaptation to market changes.

3. Resourcefulness:

Maximizing Limited Resources: Entrepreneurs typically have limited marketing budgets, so they must be resourceful, using low-cost or no-cost strategies to generate maximum impact.

Bootstrapping: Many entrepreneurial ventures rely on bootstrapping, where they use internal cash flow to fund marketing efforts rather than seeking external investment.

4. Agility and Flexibility:

Rapid Adaptation: Entrepreneurial marketing is characterized by its agility. Entrepreneurs can quickly pivot their marketing strategies in response to market feedback, competition, or changes in the business environment.

Real-Time Decision Making: Unlike larger corporations that may take time to change strategies, entrepreneurs can make decisions and implement changes quickly, often in real-time.

5. Focus on Value Creation:

Value Proposition: A clear and compelling value proposition is at the heart of entrepreneurial marketing. Entrepreneurs must clearly communicate what sets their product or service apart and why customers should choose it.

Customer Value: The focus is on creating value for customers, which in turn drives customer satisfaction, loyalty, and word-of-mouth referrals.

Entrepreneurial Marketing Strategies:

1. Guerrilla Marketing:

Guerrilla marketing involves using creative, unexpected tactics to promote a product or service. This might include flash mobs, street art, or viral social media campaigns.

Guerrilla marketing is an unconventional and creative marketing strategy that seeks to achieve maximum exposure with minimal resources. It often involves surprising or engaging the audience in unexpected ways, creating a memorable brand experience.

Key Tactics:

Street Marketing: Utilizing public spaces like sidewalks, bus stops, or parks to create eye-catching installations, murals, or flash mobs.

Viral Campaigns: Crafting content designed to be shared widely across social media platforms, often with the goal of creating a viral effect.

Pop-Up Events: Hosting temporary, surprise events in high-traffic areas to generate buzz and attract new customers.

Example: A local coffee shop might use chalk art on sidewalks to guide people to their store or host a pop-up event in a busy area to attract attention.

2. Content Marketing:

Creating valuable, relevant content to attract and engage a target audience. This might include blogs, videos, podcasts, and infographics.

Content marketing involves creating and distributing valuable, relevant, and consistent content to attract and engage a specific target audience. The goal is to build trust, establish authority, and ultimately drive profitable customer actions.

Key Tactics:

Blogging: Writing articles that address the pain points, interests, or questions of the target audience.

Video Content: Producing how-to videos, tutorials, interviews, or storytelling pieces that resonate with viewers.

Infographics: Creating visually appealing infographics that simplify complex information and make it easily digestible

Example: A startup could launch a blog offering industry insights or how-to guides related to their product, positioning themselves as thought leaders.

3. Social Media Marketing:

Social media marketing leverages platforms like Facebook, Instagram, Twitter, LinkedIn, and TikTok to connect with customers, promote products or services, and build a brand community. It is a cost-effective way to reach a large audience and engage with them directly.

Key Tactics:

Engagement Posts: Regularly posting content that encourages interaction, such as questions, polls, or challenges.

Influencer Collaborations: Partnering with influencers who have a significant following in the target market to promote products.

Social Media Advertising: Using paid ads on social platforms to target specific demographics with tailored messages.

Example: An entrepreneur might use Instagram to showcase product images, share customer stories, and interact with followers, building a loyal community.

4. Influencer Marketing:

Influencer marketing involves partnering with individuals who have a large and engaged following on social media or other platforms. These influencers promote the entrepreneur's products or services to their audience, leveraging their credibility and reach.

Key Tactics:

Product Reviews: Sending products to influencers for them to review and share their honest opinions with their followers.

Sponsored Content: Paying influencers to create and share content that highlights the entrepreneur's offerings.

Takeovers: Allowing an influencer to "take over" the brand's social media account for a day, engaging directly with the audience

Example: A beauty startup might collaborate with a popular beauty blogger to review and promote their products.

5. Referral Programs:

Referral marketing encourages existing customers to refer new customers to the business, often in exchange for incentives such as discounts, freebies, or cash rewards. It leverages the power of word-of-mouth to grow the customer base.

Key Tactics:

Referral Programs: Creating a formal program where customers earn rewards for each successful referral.

Affiliate Marketing: Partnering with individuals or other businesses to promote products, where they earn a commission for each sale generated through their referral link.

Customer Testimonials: Encouraging satisfied customers to share their positive experiences on social media or review sites.

Example: A SaaS company might offer a month of free service for every new customer referred by an existing customer.

6.Email marketing

Email marketing involves sending targeted messages directly to a subscriber's inbox, aiming to nurture relationships, promote products, and drive conversions. It is one of the most direct forms of communication with potential and existing customers.

Key Tactics:

Newsletters: Regularly sending updates, news, and valuable content to keep the audience informed and engaged.

Promotional Emails: Sending special offers, discounts, or product launches to encourage immediate action.

Automated Drip Campaigns: Setting up a series of automated emails that guide subscribers through a sales funnel, from awareness to purchase.

Importance of Entrepreneurial Marketing:

Building Brand Awareness: Entrepreneurial marketing helps new ventures create a brand presence in the market, even with limited resources.

Driving Growth: By focusing on value creation and customer engagement, entrepreneurial marketing can drive sustainable growth and build a loyal customer base.

Competitive Advantage: Creative and innovative marketing strategies can help entrepreneurs stand out in crowded markets, giving them a competitive edge.

Challenges of Entrepreneurial Marketing:

Limited Resources: Entrepreneurs often have to market their products with limited budgets, requiring them to be extremely resourceful and creative.

Market Saturation: Standing out in a crowded marketplace can be difficult, especially for new ventures with no established brand presence.

Time Constraints: Entrepreneurs often juggle multiple roles, leaving limited time for focused marketing efforts.